Am I Going To Be OK?

Achieving Financial Comfort in Today's World

Am I Going To Be OK?

Achieving Financial Comfort in Today's World

Francis D'Andrade

PER CAPITA PUBLISHING

Library and Archives Canada Cataloguing in Publication

D'Andrade, Francis, 1961–
Am I going to be ok? : achieving financial comfort in today's world / Francis D'Andrade.

ISBN-13: 978-0-9739375-0-3
ISBN-10: 0-9739375-0-5

1. Finance, Personal. I. Title.

HG179.D349 2006 332.024 C2006-905053-8

Francis D'Andrade
Per Capita Publishing
50 Minthorn Blvd., Suite 103
Markham ON L3T 7X8
www.amigoingtobeok.com

Text Design and Page Layout: Heidy Lawrance Associates, hlacreative.com

Cover Design: The Backroom Agency, thebackroomagency.com

10 09 08 07 06 1 2 3 4 5

Printed and bound in Canada

For Lisa, Garrett and Lauren

Contents

ACKNOWLEDGEMENTS

This book was made possible by the contributions of many friends and associates. I am especially grateful to Louis Delamarter for helping shape many of the concepts in the book.

Thanks to Bruce Cohen for looking over my outline and assuring me that there was an interesting book there. Doreen Miller, Reza Samahin and Brian Smith were extremely generous with their time and kept me focused and moving along whenever I got stuck. It's always nice to hear that you're not crazy.

For a guy who doesn't know anything about money and doesn't care either Greg Miron did a great job cleaning up my first draft. Bruce McDougall performed surgery to the manuscript and polished it into a readable book. I am very fortunate to have found a wonderful illustrator like John Fraser to bring many of the personal experiences and anecdotes to life.

Many thanks go out to the friends, neighbours and colleagues who indulged me by reading the manuscript: Mike Banwell, Paul Butler, Jonathan Chevreau, Colleen Davie, Valerie Grier, Chris Hodgson, Dwarka and Rawn Lakhan, Mike Levy, Randal Lichtfield, Oriana Melo, Judy Nogueira, Gerry O'Connor, Ellen Roseman, Bob Scott, Eileen Stewart and Charles Worth.

I am grateful for the patience of my colleagues at RGI Financial: Rex Chan, Kevin Chong, Tina Jakma, Paul Kalmin, Philip Kung and Allen Szeto. Special thanks to our assistant Jennifer Wong for being good at all of the things that I am not. You all did a great job holding the fort while I was away writing.

I am deeply indebted to everyone, near and far, who is involved in the farming, processing and distribution of coffee. This book would surely not have been possible without your noble contribution.

INTRODUCTION

Throughout my career I have had the opportunity to deal with many very wealthy, richly unhappy people. Sometimes it seemed the more money they had the more miserable they were. But they weren't all like that. Some of them "got it". For those who did, the getting was extremely good on the financial and emotional fronts.

On the other end of the scale, I've met lots of people who did not have much money. Many were comfortable and contented, while others saw no hope of elevating their situation. They were resigned to a life of just getting by.

If more money equals more happiness, why had I witnessed happiness and misery at every level of the economic spectrum? I concluded that financial security and peace of mind had to be about more than just money.

Let's back up a little bit here and talk about how I came to write a book about money. A few years ago I experienced a personal crisis: I paid off my mortgage. For most people this is a good thing, but for me it caused anxiety, and I didn't know why. My parents raised me to believe that when you became an adult you bought a house and then you worked to pay if off. When you achieved that goal you were free and clear. After that, your financial life was gravy and you would experience that elusive peace of mind we all want. So it bothered me… a lot. I had achieved a major financial milestone, but was not feeling the heralded sense of fulfillment.

This got me seriously thinking about the emotional side of financial security. How do we truly achieve it? It also sparked a personal quest to discover why I felt the way I did. Where was the peace of mind that was rightfully mine?

When I looked at other financial books I discovered that apparently one of the best ways to get rich may be to write a book about how to get rich. Stand in front of the personal finance section of the local bookstore and you will see that most of the books have the words 'Wealth', 'Rich', or 'Millionaire' boldly stated in the title. Their general premise is that more money equals more happiness. And, to no surprise to the buyer each book has the best method or scheme for making you deliriously rich. These books hype superior systems embodied in five rules, five steps, six steps, seven steps, seven decisions, 12 steps, or anywhere from 30 to 365 ways for achieving greater wealth and, therefore, greater happiness. Lots of people buy these books. Some actually try to implement the techniques in them, but most do not modify their financial behaviour at all after reading them. Why? The prickly thought of behavior modification is far less embraceable than the tantalizing pitch to get rich quick.

When I started writing the book I had lofty goals of shattering fixed ways of thinking and preconceived ideas. I wanted to cut through patterned formulas and change the way we look at the world and ourselves, at least with respect to money and our personal finances. 'Planned disturbance', as a friend of mine calls it. Along the journey of writing this book, my ambitions changed. In the end I've tried to write a book that anybody can benefit from regardless of his level of financial acumen or her level of wealth. Not a "how to" book about getting rich, but rather a "what to" book about what you can do to feel more financially secure.

The first part of the book is purely diagnostic and deals with a lot of theory. We'll look at some of the more common money principles that many of us believe and live by. Powerful social, cultural, and environmental forces have shaped each of our views and attitudes toward money. The validity of some of the more common notions surrounding financial security, peace of mind, and their effect on our level of overall contentment will be examined. We'll see that wealth is about constantly striving for more, but true prosperity is about having enough.

The second part of the book is more practical. We will explore a simple framework that anyone can use to achieve a greater sense of financial security. We'll see how securing your income, establishing a savings plan, owning your home and planning for retirement are crucial for achieving financial security. So hang in there if you are looking for a process that you can put into practice.

In the last section, we will look at a few of the money maxims or principles that we look to or that subconsciously guide our financial decision-making. Some are harmless, while others can be destructive to our long-term financial security.

At the very end I have included a small workbook which I hope will help you along your path to financial comfort.

The value of any instructional book lies in its capacity either to teach you something you did not already know or to show you something you already knew from a different perspective. The latter is my goal for this book. I would like you to think about financial security in terms other than wealth, because we can't all be rich. I don't want to make you an expert in the financial world. It's too complex, and the average income earner doesn't have the time or the resources to gain such expertise. And let's face it: finance can bore you to death. My goal is to reach you long before that happens. This book will give you a framework from which to consider your own feelings about money. The outcome will be to feel more financially and personally secure.

I chose the title *Am I Going to Be OK?* for this book because everyone I spoke with wanted the answer to this question.

I

EVERYTHING KILLS YOU

Why are we feeling so vulnerable?

On New Year's Eve 1999 we all had an appointment with disaster. The years leading up to that date were a period of great trepidation and countless hours of preparation. At midnight the dreaded Y2K monster was going to cause havoc throughout the world. To those of us who were not techies it sounded like some surreal revenge-of-the-machines movie was upon us—without the cheap effects. For many years we had neglected them, cursed at them when they didn't work, used them as a foot stool, spilled countless cups of coffee on them. Now it was going to be their turn. For all the neglect and abuse they had endured, they were going to shut down our lives. It was payback time. The head of our IT department was buying gold in case the worst happened. Techies did not make New Year's party plans that year. Most had to wait at the office for the seething monster. We luddites were told to turn our computers off and go home. People were stockpiling food and water. Cars were fueled for the inevitable post-apocalyptic drive. Then we sat… and waited, with one eye open. The appointed time came and absolutely nothing happened.

The big end-of-the-century bang turned out to be a whimper because we underestimated how well we had prepared for it. If left to its devices the millennium bug, as some were calling it, may have caused the terrible mayhem that many had forecast. Many doomsayers exploited our fears while building their reputations to sell books and consulting services. Many of them made a fortune catering to our fear of the unknown. We hired these experts to advise our businesses, rehearsed our disaster recovery plans and prepared our contact information. And we were continually reminded there was no such thing as 100% certainty. Although we went home feeling pretty confident that we had minimized the potential damage we still unplugged everything from the toaster to the electric toothbrush on New Year's Eve—just in case. Having been involved in the Y2K project at work I learned a lot about fear and what it takes to prepare for the unknown to minimize or eliminate its impact. I'm already thinking about my Y3K preparations. The way things are going with genomics I think I have a shot at it. I certainly have the candles.

FEAR ITSELF

We all feel a little more vulnerable than we used to. Surveys show that we are afraid of just about everything. Worse still, there seems to be a never-ending inventory of new and progressively more frightening things for us to worry about with each passing year. Was it always like this or has some new confluence of circumstances created a new order against which we have to be constantly on guard? It was a simpler time just a generation ago. All we had to worry about were those pesky Russians, urban crime, and killer

bees. The threats to our safety were much more identifiable and generally agreed upon. We knew what we were dealing with, and it seemed we could mentally prepare ourselves much better for those threats to our sense of security. Now it seems that anything could come at us from anywhere. Consequently, we are much less sure how to protect ourselves. This is new territory for us. There's nothing quite so frightening as the unknown.

In the past few years we've seen terrorism strike alarmingly close to home. We worry about where and when the next attack will occur. We live through orange alerts and red alerts. Getting on an airplane takes a little longer than it used to: With more thorough security checks, we sometimes have to remove our shoes and belt before we proceed down the ramp. No matter where we are in the world we are reminded that we could be the target of an attack. We are told that this is not a temporary situation, but a stark reality of the new world we live in.

Going outside can kill you as we learn from advisories about traffic accidents and severe weather. We've seen the damage even low-level hurricanes not to mention category five storms can cause. Going to the beach can kill us. Mosquitoes don't just light and bite anymore. They carry the West Nile virus that can kill us in a matter of days if our immune systems are weak. Do we even dare discuss chickens?

One of the biggest threats to our security in the electronic age is identity theft. My wife and I both had our credit cards compromised in the same week. We lost no money but we were inconvenienced by having to sign affidavits and change payment instructions at a number of institutions. With the help of unscrupulous lawyers, criminals can mortgage our houses or even sell them from under us. The internet has given criminals opportunities to compromise our financial security without ever meeting us or knowing who we are. Legitimate businesses unwittingly sell our personal information to parties who use it to profit illegally. Financial institutions mistakenly send our account information to other parties or dispose of our records without properly destroying them. All of this leaves us financially vulnerable.

Our levels of stress have soared as we juggle work and family obligations. Work and family commitments devour our precious time and deplete our scarce resources. We neglect ourselves as we try to manage children and parents simultaneously. And tasks that others used to do, from sorting our garbage to making coffee at work, now fall into our laps.

In the midst of it all, we may not actually be more vulnerable than we used to be, but we sure *feel* more vulnerable.

PERCEPTION IS REALITY

There was a time when the news media resembled a town crier. Advertising was a sign in a shop window. We used to read our news in the morning and watch it in the evening. Now we get it wherever we are, as long as we're conscious. The messages start when we get up, continue when we get in the car, walk down the street, and ride in an elevator. When we step out of the elevator we find a television in the reception area, another in the office and a third one in the boardroom. We can log on to our computers and get a fix and check our Blackberries for more. If anything happens anywhere we know about it instantly and are repeatedly reminded of it.

There is the perception among the public that news coverage is generally negative. If it Bleeds It Leads. My wife won't watch the news and seldom picks up a newspaper anymore. She says the news is just too depressing. Story after story… the same bad news over and over again. No wonder our level of discomfort continues to rise.

TELLING STORIES

Media outlets compete for our attention. The way you build a relationship with viewers, readers, and listeners is through emotion. The way you build emotion is by telling stories. When you present the facts you aim for the head. When you tell a story you aim for the heart. In the process, we have become emotionally invested in these stories. Not only do we feel as though we know the people involved, we also feel that the same terrible things could happen to us. We have all become risk managers, whether we like it or not.

The daily news used to report on the events of the day. This meant giving the viewer or reader the facts. The news is now told with a lot more emotion than in the past. Every news event is now a news "story". Every reporter is a frustrated novelist, screenwriter, or at the very least, columnist. Facts are impersonal and in order to create an identity for their product branding has come to the news. As a result, newsroom editors, feature writers and reporters have resorted to storytelling.

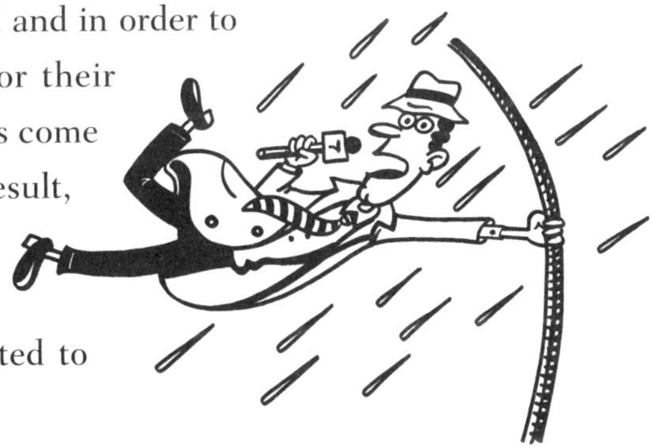

The news has become a constant din, a ringing in our ears that never seems to go away. Once upon a time I came, I saw, I conquered. Today, I sit, I watch, I wince…then go to bed and forget to floss.

More than ever we take no chances and we play the odds, however small, because we all want to manage our greater perceived vulnerability. We try to manage the risk in our lives by looking for guarantees and assurances. The more reassurance we seek the more anxious and depressed we become when we don't find it. No wonder anti-depressants have become the drug of choice. There are even doggy psychologists just in case Rover gets a little down in the snout.

And it will just get worse. The certainties that contributed to our sense of security in the past, like a steady job, a guaranteed pension, and a secure marriage are less certain now. For those of us who fear change and can't adapt, our unease and insecurity will just get worse.

BACK TO THE FUTURE

Years ago futurists promised that work would be made easier by automation. We would work fewer hours with less stress. But it didn't happen. Instead, we work longer hours, take work home and wake up in the middle of the night to get more work done. We take calls on our mobile phones during the children's soccer match and forward our calls when we go to the grocery store. A recent survey by Ipsos-Reid found that a third of us check in on work while we're on vacation. There is no escape. Wherever we are... we can be reached.

Many of us try to deal with our stress by simplifying our lives and withdrawing from the world. We retreat back to the comfort of the past which we regard as a simpler time. In the past, things were more certain. We felt more comfortable with ourselves and our prospects.

Today we don't have to leave the safety of our home anymore if we don't want to. We shut the doors, pull the blinds, turn on the TV and call it cocooning. As the world outside seems to get more complicated and dangerous, many of us can effectively work from home, bank from home and shop for groceries and other necessities from home. Yet what kind of life can we lead in a bubble? How can we enjoy our lives if we stop interacting with people and experiencing the world beyond our front

door? How can we experience real comfort and security if we let our phobias control our behaviour?

Money Phobia

If we fear something excessively or unreasonably we have a phobia. Phobias are quite common, and most people have at least one. A phobia can encompass a small universe, like entomophobia, the fear of insects. Or it can be very specific, like arachnophobia, the fear of spiders. A number of phobias relate specifically to the area of money and investing. Some of them are minor and cause only mild discomfort, while others are more severe, causing anxiety or panic attacks. Here is a small sample of the more common money phobias that I've detected among us:

Prosperphobia The fear of money.

Squirrelaphobia The fear of saving money.

Taxaphobia The fear of paying too much tax.

Auditorphobia The fear that you can never fully relax until seven years has passed.

Stockmarketphobia The fear that everybody but you makes money.

Brokerphobia The fear of investment jargon.

Annualstatementphobia The fear of opening mail in early January.

Plastiphobia The fear of credit card bills.

Insuraphobia The fear that bad things could happen to you for which you will have to sign documents that you don't understand and will never read.

Dogfoodaphobia The fear of outliving your money

Our fears can take an enormous toll on the quality of our lives. They can affect our health, family and career among other things. Commonly, we try to escape from our fears by avoiding the things or situations that trigger our anxiety. But this will not make them go away. In fact, it just means we have Confrontaphobia, which is a fear of facing our fears. Instead of trying to escape from our fears, we can do something much more effective: We can identify the source of our fear, define it and devise a plan to eliminate it.

This is what many self-directed investors have done. At one time anyone with a telephone, a pencil and the financial pages from the newspaper could make money by investing in the stock market. When that time ended, some investors got frightened and withdrew into paralysis. The smart ones set a goal and put in place a plan to achieve it.

"I'M A PENSIONER"

Last holiday my wife sends the kids and me to the grocery store to get a few items and then to the mall to pick out a Christmas tree. While in the grocery store, I see an elderly woman ahead of me in the check out line. Among other things, she has picked up a small package of chives, which has no price on it. She asks the clerk to do a price check on the chives and is told they cost $2. A pained expression comes across her face. She says "no, thank you", and then pays for her other items before leaving. I want to offer to pay for the item but do not want to embarrass her.

An hour later we're picking out a Christmas tree in the shopping mall parking lot. The elderly man who works in the lot every year makes a fresh cut to the trunk of the tree. He helps me load it in the back of the new family minivan. Admiring the automatic rear door, he says the car must be expensive. I inform him that it's not a lot of money and tell him what I paid for the vehicle. He looks at me in horror and says "I'm a pensioner". On the way home

I think about these two incidents and how much money I blow during the course of an average week without a second thought… and I am ashamed.

It occurs to me that we spend an awful lot of time worrying about things that will likely never affect us and not enough time thinking about the things that definitely will. By far, the number-one reason we save and invest is for our retirement. Although we all hope for a comfortable retirement we don't put enough effort into preparing for it. As a result many of us will have to worry about just getting by and we will not be able to enjoy some of the simple pleasures in life. Others will have to supplement their income well into their old age. If we diverted just a little of the energy that we expend worrying about remote possibilities to the real challenges that confront us, we'd have a much greater chance of overcoming those challenges. The emotional stakes are a lot higher now. Everyone is inching closer to retirement, and none of us can afford to get it wrong.

SQUARE ONE

Although, everything may not really kill you it can sure feel that way sometimes. It used to be that whatever didn't kill you made you stronger. Now it feels as though; whatever does not kill you may just drive you crazy and leave you feeling extremely vulnerable.

In the next part of the book we'll deconstruct how we think about money and financial security and look into why we don't always make the choices that maximize our success and happiness.

The way to achieve financial security in a world where you feel vulnerable is to be prepared. Being prepared means taking stock of where you are and where you want to go, and then putting in place a process for getting there. It also means continually asking one simple question: "What can go wrong?'

In the coming chapters we will outline the plans that you can implement today to achieve a better sense of financial security now and in the future.

Summary

- We feel more vulnerable than ever
- We see the future as a threat
- We worry about the wrong things
- We need to look at things rationally
- We can't let our worry distract us from the really important things.

II

WEALTH IS ABOUT *MORE*; PROSPERITY IS ABOUT *ENOUGH*

The role of money in our lives

A few years ago, I asked my five-year-old daughter how we got money to pay for things. She said that daddy went to work. Then I asked her what daddy did to earn the money. She said daddy went to work and ran on a treadmill until money came out of it.

At the tender age of five, my daughter had already nailed the concept of work: We run on a treadmill, and money comes out of it. If there were an international symbol for work, wouldn't it be a treadmill?

This little episode with my daughter got me thinking more about how we relate to money. How much was nature and how much was nurture? Did we have some innate ability to deal with money? Was it a matter of biology or sociology? How much did we learn from our environment and from our social, cultural, and familial realms?

HUMAN NURTURE

I didn't have to wait long to test the nature-versus-nurture question. A little while later, my daughter's Girl Scout group held a career day. They asked me to come and talk about money. I was going to beg off, but my wife was the group leader, and I had no excuse. When the evening came, I ransacked my son's fledgling currency collection and scored a US dollar, a Kenyan shilling and a five-Euro bill. Off I went to the local school gymnasium.

I felt pretty good about my contribution to the evening's exercise until I realized the parent ahead of me worked at a chewing gum company. My "rival" came armed with a bag full of Dubble Bubble. The kids were still buzzing about the free gum and chewing with delight when I walked to the center of the gymnasium and handed out the currency that I'd lifted from my son's collection. As the girls passed around the money, I asked, "Does anybody know where money comes from?" Every hand shot up, and I thought maybe this wouldn't be such a disaster after all. According to the Girls Scouts, money came from a wallet or from mom. Then I asked how we earn the money. The first girl said, "I make my bed." The next girl said, "I'm nice to my brother". The third girl gave my favorite answer— "I lose a tooth".

These experiences convinced me that our relationship with money has more to do with nurture than nature. Our beliefs about money depend on our experience of money. I resolved to do a better job teaching my children about money, mainly by example. If I set a good example of how to handle money, perhaps they won't be living in my basement in their 30s.

NOT YOUR FAULT

About fifteen years ago, I worked for a direct-to-public mutual-fund company that ran an ad of Joe Louis, the legendary boxer, saying, "I don't like money actually, but it quiets my nerves". It generated an incredible response. Most people have had an uneasy experience with money and can relate to the anxiety that money arouses. Money scares us because we don't understand it, so my company promised to help people understand the complex world of finance, investments and money.

Handling money does not come naturally to us. We have to learn how to deal with it, just as we did when humans first developed the concept. Eons ago, we survived off the land. We crawled into a cave and threw a skin over our backs for warmth. We picked berries from the land and ate whatever ran across our path. If the supply of food dried up, we simply packed up and went someplace else, where it was much more plentiful. If that didn't work, we perished.

As we learned to grow food and raise animals, make our own clothing and build our own shelter, we lived with more certainty. We became less nomadic and put down roots. Eventually, as we became even more specialized, we began to barter with our neighbours. However, it became cumbersome to trade 500 loaves of bread for our neighbour's prized ox.

To exchange goods more efficiently, we invented currency.

Today we think of currency as coins and bills. But a number of items have been used as currency over the ages, from beans to seashells to animal skins. All of these items had in common the value that a society attributed to them. None of these items had any value in themselves. But currency was convenient. We didn't have to compare the value of our stuff to the stuff we wanted. We simply gave or received a standard amount of shells or skins for a particular good or service.

As we expanded our horizons, we found some societies that used seashells as a currency and others that used beans. To allow for more universal trade, we came up with coins and paper whose value was guaranteed by a local government or bank. Money was now compact and non-perishable, so we could hang on to it and save it till we really needed it. This allowed us to accumulate a store of wealth that was measurable and broadly accepted. Money was also good for business. The economy took off. Cash was now king.

To relieve us of the challenge of carrying all our cash in a bag, we invented checks. Then, for people who hated carrying a checkbook, we invented credit cards. These allowed people of good standing in the community to pay for goods and services not just with their own money, but with other peoples', as well, on the assumption that they'd pay it back eventually and pay interest until they did. We have now mastered the concept of spending other people's money. It seems like everyone has a credit card now, even dogs have been known to receive credit cards.

As our trading habits continually change, so too will the form of money. We seldom carry cash any more, preferring electronic currency instead. In fact, less than 10% of the entire world's currency exists in cash. The rest exists as a bunch of debits and credits on the computer systems of banks throughout the world.

Regardless of the form it takes, many of us have a hard time grasping the concept of money, and many more of us just can't handle money very well. None of us should feel especially bad about this. We did not crawl out of the swamp with an innate ability to deal with money. All we can do is learn how to manage our money effectively. After all, we invented the stuff.

DIVINE WISDOM

I remember when I was a kid in high school the business section was only in the Thursday edition of the local newspaper. With the exception of the Wall Street Journal and The Financial Post, news about economics and finance did not make its way into the general public's consciousness until the '90s. That was when we began to take a more serious interest in investing, largely by embracing mutual funds. Usually, the more money we had riding on the market, the more interest we took in news that affected our investments.

It's hard to walk down the street now without getting an update on the markets. If you live in the city, updates are flashed from giant TV screens at intersections. The radio stations give reports on market moves every half hour. It's much like football pools; you take a greater interest when you have a little money riding on the outcome.

We now worship money. The pursuit of wealth consumes more of our thought and time than it ever has. Just as religion once dominated our lives and a church or cathedral stood on every street corner, today we can't walk down the street without passing a shrine to commerce and finance while receiving a market update on our wireless phone.

THE HAPPIEST MAN ON THE FACE OF THE EARTH

Many of us have been raised to believe that the more money we have, the more happiness we'll enjoy. Most of us don't know specifically what we want to do with it. We just know that we want lots of it, the more the better.

We admire and envy the rich and successful, and we assume they're very happy. We believe despite ourselves that, if we buy this car, these clothes, this watch, or this handbag, we will ensure our happiness. And yet we know that more money does not really bring more happiness.

There is over $4 trillion of wealth in Canada. This represents a median net worth of roughly $145,000 according to the most recent statistics. A study by Merrill Lynch and Cap Gemini estimates there are almost 400,000 millionaires in Canada. Almost 70% of the wealth in the country is controlled by just 20% of the families. That means that, if wealth is the key to happiness, then 400,000 millionaires will laugh all the way to the bank while about 80% of us may spend our lives as grumpy old Canadians.

According to Forbes Magazine, the happiest man on the face of the earth lives in Redmond, Washington, and really likes playing with gadgets. Bill Gates, co-founder of Microsoft, has topped the list of the world's wealthiest individuals for the past 12 years. If we believe more money equals exponentially more happiness, then Bill Gates is approximately 50,000 times happier than your garden-variety millionaire. Add another zero to that if you want to know how much happier he is than the average grumpy Canadian.

"I'D BE HAPPY IF I HAD A LITTLE MORE MONEY"

I wish I had a dime for every time I heard someone tell me that the only thing that stood between him and happiness was just a little more money. I've heard this from people with one dollar to their name and those who had a million. American Express asked 1,000 Canadians who earn an annual household income of $200,000 or more if they would keep working if they won a lottery. Most said they'd keep working if they won $1 million, about half said they'd quit if they won $2 million, and nine out of 10 would pack it in if they won $5 million. This would suggest that wealth would be a more important factor for well-being and financial security than income. But how would this test with people who had significant wealth?

THERE'S MONEY AND THEN THERE'S MONEY

In 2005 PNC Advisors, a wealth manager in the US did a survey of 500 wealthy Americans with more than $1 million in investable assets to see how they looked at financial security. They found that even the very wealthy worry about financial security. When asked how much they needed to feel financially secure in the future respondents consistently said that they needed approximately double their current level of assets.

Those with a half million to $1 million said they needed on average $2.4 million, those with $5 million or more needed $10.4 million on average while those with $10 million or more felt they needed a median of $18.1 million. This is rather alarming, as one has to assume that at one point those with $5 million had only $1 million and may have thought to themselves. "Gee, if I could only get another $1 million I'd be happy". But $5 million brought new anxiety and $10 million brought a full-scale panic attack. Perhaps the wealthy really are different from you and me.

Maybe life on Easy Street isn't as comfortable as you might imagine. Needing almost twice as much money to feel secure when you already have $10 million in investable assets sounds a little absurd to most people. To the average person there is no difference between $10 million and $20 million, but to the very wealthy there's money and then…there's money.

If you're thinking that all that money made them happier, if not more secure, then you'd be surprised to know that less than half (46%) said that they had become happier as they've accumulated more assets. Of those who had greater than $10 million, 29% said it brings them more problems than it solves. More astonishingly, 33% those with in excess of $10 million in investible assets said that having enough money is a constant worry in their life.

Meanwhile, studies by University of Illinois professor Edward Diener have shown that wealthy people listed in the Forbes 400 are only a tiny bit happier than the rest of us. Wealth is relative, and even the very wealthy may feel a few bucks shy of happiness.

All this goes to show that with added wealth come added complications, demands and worries. We all know that the more we get, the more we seem to want. We also know that the secret to peace of mind may be to stop wanting more when we achieve a reasonable level of prosperity.

All of this made me wonder what money really means for our sense of security and happiness. I needed to understand why paying my mortgage, although gratifying was not the financial nirvana I had imagined. It felt good, but I hadn't fully grasped that I would soon make this feeling the norm.

THICK AND THIN

It's hard to make decisions that maximize our happiness when we don't really know what makes us happy in the first place. Research by Harvard psychology professor Daniel Gilbert shows that we often predict incorrectly how we'll feel after a particular experience. We tend to overestimate the intensity and duration of our feelings after positive and negative events. The pleasant feelings we associate with achieving or acquiring something will likely not be as intense or as lasting as we anticipate. Conversely, we will likely not feel the effect of a setback as strongly or for as long as we expect. We have a tendency to make the unusual feel normal. This also means that we probably make financial decisions based on inaccurate expectations of their effect on our well-being.

According to Gilbert, we also tend to forget that we will overestimate the impact of our decisions on our future well-being. Therefore, we will go on making the same mistake in judgment over and over again. Just ask the celebrity couples who keep getting married, over and over again. After the eighth marriage, you'd think they'd get it. But I guess they just keep forgetting how miserable the last seven marriages have made them.

So how efficiently do we make decisions that maximize our happiness? The new luxury item that we yearn for may provide us with an emotional lift, but will it be as intense or last as long as we expect? Perhaps this explains why I didn't feel as good as I thought I would when I paid off my mortgage. It also makes me wonder if the decisions we make today about our retirement will deliver the intended level of happiness tomorrow.

CLIMATE CONTROL

We have a natural ability to adjust to changes in our circumstances. When something unfamiliar happens to us, we make it familiar. Psychologists refer to this as adaptation. Out of self-preservation, we can make bad events feel not so bad and good events feel not so good. By smoothing out life's twists and turns we achieve a balance that allows us to carry on through thick and thin.

It happens in our financial lives. Lottery winners quickly adapt to the positive change in their wealth. Some of them even spend themselves back to their old lifestyle. Alternatively, when financial hardship hits, we try to keep our circumstances constant until we recover or adjust. Executives who lose their jobs may move from a house they own to a rented house in the same neighbourhood, but they'll also try to preserve their status by continuing club memberships and keeping the kids in the same private schools for as long as they can.

So how do we figure out what will make us happy in the future if we have such a high propensity to predict incorrectly the outcome of our choices? I suppose the answer starts with a firm grasp of what truly makes us happy in the first place.

GIDDY WITH GLEE

For most of us, happiness is a subjective state of well-being that doesn't depend on any single factor. And we're all different. One person's happiness may be another person's nightmare.

Periodically I ask my kids if they're happy. They usually give me their standard "yeah, dad, I'm always happy" answer. But I won't let them off the hook so easily. I usually ask them what specifically they're happy about, hoping they'll feel grateful for their good fortune. I also ask them what they'd change in their lives if they could. (Preventing their dad from periodically asking them stupid questions doesn't count.) What would make them happier? Regardless of their answers, I never want them to forget that one of the objectives in life is happiness.

For me, happiness comes with those fleeting and unforeseen moments when I stop and think "wow… that's amazing". I also find happiness in memories of positive experiences. I could be just hanging out with the kids at the seaside as they pile sand on my head. Or walking the dog through the trails near my house after work as I decompress while losing myself in the scenery. For others, happiness comes from driving their car through the countryside with the windows down and the radio playing the perfect song at just the right moment. Maybe its baby's first steps, or a neighbour's invitation to a barbecue. Our happiness usually comes from simple pleasures that don't cost a lot of money.

UTILITY AT THE MARGIN

Economists know we need to expend a certain amount of energy to feel happy and fulfilled, but the expenditure of additional units of energy will diminish the effect. They call this marginal utility. There is a point where the value derived from some activity isn't worth the energy required to produce it.

We might eat an ice cream cone and feel very happy. We think we'll feel twice as happy if we eat another one. By the sixth cone we don't feel so good at all. And eating another cone wouldn't be worth the effort.

In the world of money rather than ice cream, marginal utility is a function of our expectations and our social surroundings. But at the end of the day, we ourselves determine our optimal level of happiness and decide how much energy or money we need to achieve it.

I'M HAPPY AREN'T I?

The good news is that we're already rich. By that, I mean rich relative to other countries in the world and relative to past standards. The bad news is that we're no happier for it. By every economic measure we're a much wealthier society today than we've ever been. North Americans enjoy one of the highest per-capita standards of living in the world. The United Nations consistently ranks Canada as one of the finest places on the planet to live. After WW II about one-third of Americans described themselves as "very happy". Since then, subjective happiness scores have barely budged even though we've all become far wealthier.

Don't get me wrong; I have nothing against wealth. It's just not the all-encompassing objective of the game. Many things that don't involve money influence our levels of happiness and contentment, including our personal relationships and our physical, mental and spiritual condition. If we happen to get wealthy as we strive for financial security, then fine, we'll deal with it. But if our goal is financial security, then wealth itself isn't necessary. It can even be a distraction.

Summary

- Our sense of money is not innate.
- We need to learn how to handle money.
- We worship money.
- Wealth is not a guarantee of happiness or security.
- True financial security is an emotional threshold.

III

SEE AND NOT BE SEEN

We have a primal need to feel secure

If I had to write my personal statement of belief it would have something to do with balance. My version of the Cartesian cogito would be something like "I balance, therefore I am." Throughout my life, I've taken this approach to almost everything I do. It sounds kind of boring but it has kept me on an even keel. I don't care for big highs, and I loathe big lows. Balance embodies the essence of what I am. It is what I naturally strive for in my personal and professional life; how I achieve a level of comfort that

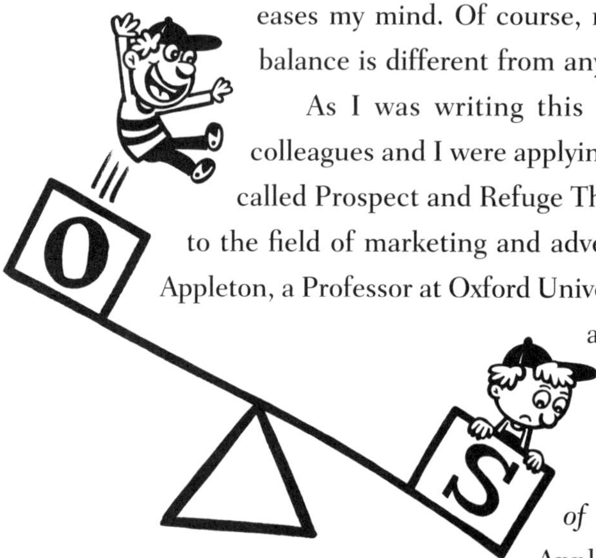

eases my mind. Of course, my sense of balance is different from anyone else's.

As I was writing this book some colleagues and I were applying a concept called Prospect and Refuge Theory (PRT) to the field of marketing and advertising. Jay Appleton, a Professor at Oxford University, wrote a book about it in 1975 called, *Experience of Landscape*. Appleton loves landscape paintings and collects them. He believes that we appreciate landscape scenes because each of us has a innate ability to look at a landscape and immediately see the opportunity and the safety.

Over the years PRT has been applied to landscape design, architecture and other disciplines. It struck me as particularly relevant to financial services, since much of what we do in this area involves reward and risk. As we do when we look at a landscape scene, we look at our financial lives with a desire to balance opportunity and safety. We want to hide ourselves away from risk while hunting for the rewards. We want to see but not be seen. To see the hunting ground from the safety of the cave is the ultimate expression of fulfillment. When I ask prospective clients what they want to achieve many jokingly reply that they want big returns with no risk. But in an increasingly complex world it seems we've lost our ability to distinguish clearly the risks from the rewards. As a result we fall short of maximizing our financial happiness.

KEEP A LEVEL HEAD

So far, we've tenuously defined happiness. We've shown that happiness does not depend on wealth. We've seen that, in our expectations of feeling happy, we sometimes make bad decisions, over and over again. We've seen that we all have a strong desire to feel secure. If our happiness depends on a sense of security rather than an accumulation of wealth, then perhaps we need to take a new approach to a secure financial life.

A basic premise of this book is: Wealth is about more, prosperity is about enough. To me, wealth means the acquisition of more money relative to other people. Prosperity suggests comfort, contentment, peace of mind and happiness. We find prosperity when we achieve a personal balance.

Just as I have my own sense of balance, I believe we all have a natural point of comfort. It may not stay in one place throughout our lives. It may fluctuate according to our age, experience or particular situation. But all of us recognize the point where we feel a sense of equilibrium. When we ignore this point of equilibrium, we get out of sorts, physically, mentally, spiritually and financially.

Each of us has the capacity to maintain an optimal balance between opportunity and safety, fulfillment and stability. But it's not easy, especially in a culture that constantly reinforces that more wealth equals more happiness. If we embrace this message too enthusiastically, we extend ourselves too far beyond our comfort zone. We lose our balance. We become unglued. Unlike wealth, prosperity involves achieving a sense of personal financial balance. Rather than accumulating wealth, our work in progress becomes maintaining our balance.

HOW MUCH IS ENOUGH?

Our ultimate sense of security comes when we feel that we have enough. We feel that we have enough when we reach the point where opportunity and security balance most favorably. Each of us has a different point of ideal balance. At no point does our sense of financial security depend on someone else's. My prosperity may be your poverty.

There is no easy way to identify our precise point of balance. We're dealing after all with emotion. Like a great landscape painting or great art in general, we'll know it when we see it. We also know when we've missed the point. With too much security, for example, we may never leave the house. With too much opportunity, we may never stop striving for more. Balance is the key. Every person who has ever consulted me for financial counseling has an optimal comfort level, where he or she finds enough safety to remain calm and enough opportunity to feel fulfilled. Too much of one or the other upsets the balance altogether.

MOTIVATED BY NEEDS

One of the most widely accepted theories of human motivation was advanced by psychologist Abraham Maslow. He presented his hierarchy of needs not as a finished work, but as an untested theory that he hoped others would take up and develop further.

Maslow believed that humans are motivated by needs, but he also believed that some needs are more urgent than others. In Maslow's hierarchy of needs, we take care of our basic needs first and leave the rest for later.

Our physiological needs come first: food, water and a hat to keep us warm. For a hungry man, the choice between a sandwich and a BMW is a no brainer in Maslow's world.

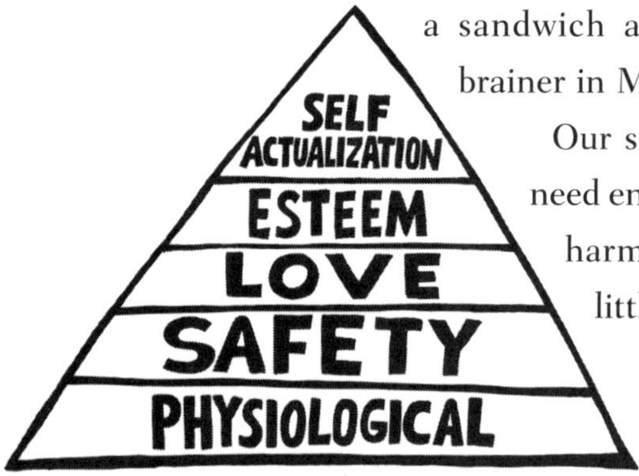

Our safety comes next. We need enough to feel free from harm. The BMW is still a little way off.

Third, we need love and companionship. Friendships, marriage, family, and community play a big role in our emotional health and protect us from loneliness and isolation. If all else fails, get a dog. But still no BMW.

Maslow referred to these first three basic needs as deficiency needs. You do not necessarily get a big emotional lift from them but if you are deficient you have to go back and fill the vessel before resuming your climb up the hierarchy of needs.

We spend much of our time attending to our needs at these three levels. Food, clothing, shelter, friends, a spouse and a dog. What more can a body want? Esteem, that's what. Esteem involves our ego and the satisfaction we derive from power, prestige, or achievement. Maslow distinguished two levels of esteem; the respect and adoration of others and the higher need of self-respect. A feeling of self-worth is more important than the recognition of others, but it's much harder to attain. Do you lease that BMW to impress your friends or buy it because you love good cars?

At the fifth and final level comes self-actualization. We need to feel a sense of personal development and express our creativity. According to Maslow, only a few people among us, perhaps as few as two per cent, have the capacity to achieve self-actualization. With respect to a great theoretician, I think self-actualization means feeling comfortable in our own skin, and I think each and every one of us can feel that way.

Maslow's hierarchy of needs can also apply to the world of personal finance. We all have basic financial needs upon which we build a foundation for our higher needs, which deliver an increasing sense of security and independence.

At the first level, we need an income. With an income, we can meet our basic needs and achieve financial independence.

At the second level, we need savings. Our savings not only keep us in the game during difficult times, they also provide us with a sense of comfort. Savings represent

both our job security fund and our future fund.

Our financial independence depends on fulfilling our needs at the first two levels. We may not die without them, but we'll certainly diminish our chances of achieving maximum happiness and fulfillment.

Next are our higher financial needs which we require for fulfillment and growth. At the third level comes home ownership. A house is the most significant non-financial asset that most of us will ever own. Not only does it satisfy our need for shelter and provide a great place to raise a family, it also provides us with safety, forces us to save, enhances our credit, appreciates tax-free, and protects us against inflation. None of this comes, by the way, from merely buying a house. The trick is to own it.

At the fourth level comes retirement. At this stage in life most of us stop working and no longer earn an income. Instead we rely on some form of long-term savings, which we can use to create a stream of income that will sustain us for the rest of our lives. Without these savings, we have to either keep working or live quite modestly.

We reach the fifth level, equivalent to Maslow's self-actualization, when we achieve financial independence and self-reliance. As I've mentioned, everyone has a different sense of autonomy and self-reliance and the financial requirements to achieve them. As in Maslow's hierarchy, we have to attend to our needs at each level before we can move higher. And as we encounter a setback, we have to satisfy our most basic needs before we resume our progress toward financial independence.

I'm sure that most people can articulate many financial needs but these are the common needs which I have observed give the greatest number of people the highest sense of security.

Summary

- We all have a primal need for opportunity and safety.
- We are motivated by needs, and some needs are more important than others.
- There's a financial hierarchy of needs, which we must follow to achieve financial security.
- Each of us has a different sense of financial security, but we can all follow a common path to achieve it.

IV

SEE THE FUTURE

Prepare to feel secure

While we don't have a primal need to feel rich, we do have a primal need to feel secure. Security may not make us happy, but we can't feel happy without security. This book explains how we can all feel more financially secure, now and in the future.

Many of us go through life without thinking about how we can get from where we are to where we want to be. We rely on fate or God to look out for us. Without knowing what will happen next, we live a life of anxiety and uncertainty. We can alleviate these feelings by taking control of our situation.

Before we take the first step toward financial security, we have to appreciate where we stand now. Once we do this, we can bring a sense of order and consistency to our financial lives. If we want to achieve something, we first have to define it, then we can plan for it, which allows us to process it and then measure our progress so that we can eventually live it. If we do all of this, then the future will more likely unfold the way we envisioned it.

Define it: Most of us have some idea of how we'd like our future to unfold. I call this our outcome, which is not some end state but the entire journey. If we don't know how we want our future to unfold then the outcome will happen purely by chance, not design. In my experience, people who don't define their goals usually just want more. If you want a specific and achievable outcome, you first have to define it. More is not a valid objective.

Plan for it: We achieve an outcome through planning and preparation. The plan is nothing but a verbal expression of our dream. If we can articulate it, we can understand it. Ideally, we should write it down. Most of us can articulate a plan that leads to a specific outcome. We're more likely to get there if we can refer to our plan in writing.

Process it: Like any other kind of planning, financial planning helps us to get from *here* to *there*. We bridge the gap by putting in place a process that we can realistically follow. This is the action part of the plan. The process lays out the specific tactics that we'll use to achieve our outcome. Unfortunately, this is where most people drop the ball.

Measure it: If I want to lose weight, I have to weigh myself. If I want to confirm my health, I have to take my temperature. If my goal is financial security, then I have to measure my progress. What gets measured gets done.

Live it: The discipline that it takes to define, plan, process and measure our financial outcome will eventually become a habit if we just do it. Discipline doesn't come naturally to us. Habits do. That makes them a lot easier to follow.

MONEY IS ENERGY

It's not enough to feel financially secure now. True financial security requires that we also feel good about the future. The only problem is that we are human beings and human nature can't seem to think past the next 10 minutes.

Too many people regard the future as a threat. Your money is really just a form of energy. You need to expend much of your energy to live in the present, but you also need to conserve a significant portion of your energy for the future. If you follow a simple process which is driven by your need for security the future will be much less of a threat.

EXCUSES EXCUSES

Financial security is an attainable outcome. But along the way, we'll probably make numerous excuses for falling short of our objective: "I'm just not good with money", "I'm not smart enough", "I don't have the time to do it properly". Don't worry. We all make these excuses from time to time.

We tend not to like budgets, and saving money seems to be a completely unnatural act. We rely on process to help us tackle challenges that we don't enjoy or that don't come naturally to us. When the process becomes a habit, the whole exercise gets easier.

In the next chapters, I will show you how to develop the habit of achieving financial security using the energy of money to keep you going.

In the next part of the book you'll see why securing your income, saving a portion of it, owning your home and planning early for retirement are the sources of financial security for so many Canadians.

Summary

- Financial security is attainable.
- To attain it, we have to define, plan, process, measure and live it.
- What starts as discipline becomes a habit.
- It's not so hard to develop the habit of contributing to our financial security.

V

EARNING AN OUTCOME

What you can do to secure your income

Like many people with a liberal arts education, I fell into my career. I wasn't big on academia, nor did I have any long-range vision. This unnerved me at times. Many other students had set goals and ambitions. I had ambitions, but they were more of the 24-hour variety. A day brought what it would. I wasn't getting anywhere, but I was having a great time going nowhere. Observing became something of a passion, and I went with it. One

circumstance led me to another. When I look back now I can't help but think, "How did I get here?" Things have turned out pretty well for me though because I've liked what I've done. Many people aren't so lucky, and they end up doing things that they don't particularly like at all.

Whether we like it or not, all of us have to make a living. That's the first and crucial step toward financial security. Many personal finance books advise us that the secret to wealth is to pay ourselves first. But none of us can do that unless we get paid in the first place.

This factor can't be overstated. Our first need is to ensure we get paid. Only then can we pay ourselves. Without an income we cannot have an outcome.

IT'S GOOD TO BE REGULAR

Most Canadians would define financial security as a reliable income. Starting with an allowance, then part-time work during school years, on to a full-time job or two (or three or four or five), and then into retirement—from a very early age we become used to receiving some form of income. Whether it's given, earned, harvested or inherited, an income has a dramatic effect on how we conduct our lives.

There are few things more comforting than a regular and constant stream of cash. Companies love cash flow, investors love cash flow, ordinary folks love cash flow, the more regular the better. It doesn't even matter how much we receive, as long as it's reliable. We need a consistent income to sustain our families and ourselves, to take care of everyday expenses along with the unexpected small and large expenses that seem occasionally to arise out of nowhere.

The security we feel about our income not only makes us feel better, it also keeps the economy going. Researchers have shown that consumer confidence depends on people's job security and employment prospects. That's what drives us to the mall, the car showroom, the fancy restaurants, the exotic resorts, and the real-estate agent. With our cash flow we look after our financial obligations and then feed most of our desires.

Our ability to move up the financial hierarchy of needs and achieve financial independence requires that we first secure an income and then save a portion of it. With that portion we can begin to build our desired outcome.

IT'S NEVER EASY

About sixty percent of all working Canadians have a traditional full-time job. The remaining forty percent of us are either self-employed, casual, part-time, temporary, seasonal, and/or contract employees. Among other things, we receive no employee benefits; our employers bear no obligations for our well-being now or in the future.

Whether we have a traditional job or a non-traditional job, most of us don't have a trust fund that will free us from financial cares or a family business that we can take over some day. Most of us have to go out into the world and earn a living. Few of us will find a job for life; working for a company that guarantees our security with reliable pay and a good pension plan.

Instead of a permanent job guaranteed by a company, we will more likely spend our careers with several companies of all sizes and possibly in many different places. As employees, we've gone from climbing ladders to jumping from one ladder to another. In the process, we've sacrificed safety for more opportunity. This dramatic shift in our comfort zone means that we face more uncertainty as we've re-framed our approach to work. So how do we find security in such a volatile environment?

Above all else, we can keep our skills up to date. In many careers, education has become the price of entry, while adding to a portfolio of skills has become our annual due.

Generally, as we age and collect more relevant skills we become more productive and, therefore, more valuable to an employer. Sometimes we don't even know that we've acquired a skill until we need to apply it. One of my clients, a software engineer, says he acquired knowledge in his career of dozens of programs that have now become obsolete. But he maintains that his experiences are still valuable because they allow him to see an outcome more quickly and waste less time. A skill we no longer use may still compliment our new skills and pay dividends even years after we acquire it.

FIT IS EVERYTHING

If we're lucky we'll be well suited to and, actually enjoy, our chosen vocation. We'll develop skills and gain experience in our field, which will allow us to enjoy a prosperous and fulfilling career. But what happens if we choose the wrong career?

Job satisfaction and job security are like happiness—largely subjective. How we feel has a lot to do with the economy, the industry that we work in, and the position we hold. Satisfaction could also depend on the functions we perform, opportunities for advancement, esteem, and the amount of money we make. Am I content doing a very specific task, or do I require variety to feel fulfilled? Do I have a great need for social interaction? There are a number of variables within each job and each company that contribute to the work environment. Each will influence our overall job satisfaction.

I once assumed responsibility for another department than my own in a corporate shake up. Once I assured the employees that their positions were secure they began to tell me more about themselves. I was astonished at the number of people who were doing things they did not want to do either because their job specs no longer described their actual work or because they'd never really wanted to do their jobs in the first place. As a result, the department was not performing efficiently, and most of the employees were unhappy.

DON'T FALL INTO A RUT

Just as wealth does not guarantee happiness and peace of mind, advancement up the corporate ladder does not guarantee job satisfaction. In fact, high achieving executives often feel less satisfied than lesser achievers. In a survey by Korn Ferry International Executive 1,700 global executives said they would recommend their career to others, but more than half would choose a different career if they could start over.

Choosing the right career, company and job brings undeniable psychological and economic benefits. One of my best employees worked for me every winter during the busy financial season, but returned to his swimming-pool maintenance business during the summer. He was a terrific advisor, with all the proper credentials, so, at the end of one season, I asked him if he'd like to stay on full-time. He said no. He preferred being outside in the summertime. He knew what he wanted to do, and he did it.

If you're not sure where your career is headed or where you would like it to lead, get help. Find a career counselor, a book, a web-based profiler to assess your values, interests, personality, and skills. Even writing down what you're good at helps to guide you toward a turning point and onto a new career path. You need to get on that path if you want to achieve an optimal level of satisfaction and security.

LOYALTY IS OLD FASHIONED

People once stayed in their jobs out of loyalty. In the past, loyalty was a virtue. Companies rewarded loyal employees with a gold watch. But in the new work environment, loyalty may be perceived as a sign of weakness and, therefore, detrimental to your career.

You can rise through the ranks slowly, or you can jump around, and get there sooner, advancing on your talent. An acquaintance of mine, the Chief Marketing Officer of a large multinational bank, firmly believes that he got where he is today by jumping to increasingly more senior positions whenever the opportunity came along. He's an extremely capable man with a long list of achievements. As he moved from one job to another, he felt confident that his ability would become readily apparent when opportunities came his way, and he did not feel that he needed the refuge of tenure.

MAKE SURE YOU'RE PROVIDING GOOD VALUE

Employees often don't realize how much their employer invests in them. Training new employees can cost several months salary while the employee is being paid to acquire new skills. The expertise that an employee develops over the years is also an investment. Knowledge of corporate strategy and relationships is a valuable asset. Employers have a lot riding on their employees. They need to see the value constantly or they'll look to eliminate the expense.

In the new world of performance based compensation companies can now readily identify the employees, departments, and divisions that are performing and the ones that aren't, and they will then make changes accordingly. There is no place to hide anymore. The most productive people will like this new environment, but the laggards will be exposed.

EDUCATION IS INCOME

Studies have shown that most kids decide to attend university before their fifteenth birthday. If you have a child who's approaching this age, you should encourage her to pursue a higher education. It could affect her earning potential and her sense of financial security for the rest of her life.

According to Statistics Canada's 2001 Census we are better educated than ever. Education levels have been rising since the Second World War, but really accelerated during the 1990s. Women especially have embraced higher education and now comprise approximately half of all university graduates. As a result, they've closed the income gap with men significantly in the past 25 years. In 1980, women earned just $0.52 for every $1 earned by males. This ratio rose to $0.64 by 2000. And young women aged 25 to 29 earn almost the same amount as their male counterparts.

Not surprisingly, higher education combined with work experience had the most favourable influence on increasing income. Approximately 60% of people in the lowest earnings category of $20,000 did not have more than a high-school education in 2000. Conversely, of those earning more than $100,000, 61% had a university degree.

As for yourself, if it's too late to attend university think about upgrading your skills through a community college or trade certification program. Statistics Canada data on income by education clearly indicate that university graduates earn more than those with college diplomas, and college graduates earn more than high-school educated employees. Any opportunity to increase your level of education is an opportunity to increase your income and financial security.

WELL SPOKEN IS WELL REGARDED

Someone once said that 90% of strategy is execution, and 90% of execution is communication. Communication and organizational skills allow us to navigate through the corporate maze with less effort while affording us the opportunities to earn optimal results. Communication skills work in any environment and travel well, just in case we move from one job to another. It's worth investing in communication skills.

Improving our communication skills also helps us to interact with clients and customers, the people who are ultimately responsible for our income. The former head of a mutual fund company once told me that one of the keys to his success was that he was reasonably well spoken. He came from a modest background in England but learned to speak the Queen's English, as they say. His mother was convinced that being well spoken was a skill her son would need to be successful in life, so she sent him to elocution lessons as a young man. He attributed a great deal of his success to his elocution. It's hard to imagine a more important business skill than the ability to communicate clearly and effectively.

FIND A MENTOR

I've always thought of a boss as a mentor whom I could learn from. In turn, I've always tried to be a mentor to the people who report to me. Not only does a mentor help your career, a mentor can also make your life easier.

According to the Hay Group, the number-one determinant of job satisfaction is your relationship with your immediate superior.

I was very fortunate to have a great boss when I was building my career in financial services. Making him look good was an important part of my job. I tried to do this by providing good ideas for improving our business. One of the ways I did this was to take the numerous proposals and reports that piled up on his desk and analyze them. He was agreeable to this, because he was too busy to read them anyway. When I put them back on his desk, I left a note indicating what I thought of the proposal and whether or not I thought it would help the organization. I made certain my comments were always well considered and concise. Soon, he started calling to let me know when he had a new pile of papers on the corner of his desk. My extra effort got me noticed.

If employees in my department did a good job and made me look good while we accomplished our tasks successfully, they would benefit as well. In the process, I made sure that they received a sound education in the inner workings of the company. I made sure they met and worked with key people inside and outside the company. My employees got to know other decision-makers since most of the projects cross-pollinated with other departments, suppliers, and consultants. In that way, they advanced their careers.

A mentor should stand further up the corporate food chain and be advancing toward a higher position. A mentor with no future won't do much for yours. As a good protégé, you also have to contribute to their position.

If your boss is not a mentor, then start looking for one. A mentor will have a big impact on your overall satisfaction and your income.

ALWAYS NETWORK

Networks of friends, family and professional associates are great sources of information. And they usually give information freely. People like being asked about their work or family life. In turn, others will ask you for information. This is how you keep the information pipeline open.

Too many people decide to start networking after they lose their job. But networking doesn't work so well when you don't have a job. To other people, you don't seem nearly as interesting or charming as you did when you worked for the big company. It's a lot easier to meet contacts when they want to meet you. After all, you're trying to share knowledge and build your reputation. When you're out of work, you're out of the loop.

BRAND YOURSELF

Like Coca Cola, Pontiac or the Gap, our colleagues and superiors regard us as a brand. The brand we convey makes a lasting impression and ultimately has a lot to do with our security and satisfaction at work. To build our brand, we should ask colleagues what they think we stand for, and listen very carefully to what they have to say. If they tell us something that we don't want to hear, then we should tell them how we'd like to be perceived and ask them how they think we can achieve this perception.

Like a brand, we represent the organization that employs us to outsiders. Our behaviour influences their perception of our organization. I once encountered a competitor who seemed very arrogant. Whenever I met people from his company, I just assumed that they were arrogant too. They may not have been arrogant but they had to convince me first.

FOR ALL APPEARANCES

A few years ago, while I was in a Paris café with my family, I happened to witness an attempted robbery. A well dressed older man walked through the café and knocked over a glass from a table. While it shattered on the floor and created a diversion, he attempted to retrieve the wallet from another customer's suit jacket that was draped on the back of the chair beside me. It all happened in an instant, and I just reacted. I immediately grabbed his arm and the thief ran out of the café. While relating what had happened to my wife, she asked what he looked like. I told her he looked just like any respectable gentleman you would encounter on any given day. This experience validated for me the notion that appearance has an enormous impact on how we perceive one another.

Daniel Hamermesh, economics professor at the University of Texas at Austin, studied the effect of appearance on success. He found that good-looking candidates had a better chance of winning an election; attractive students got more attention and higher marks, and students gave good-looking university professors higher evaluations. Other studies have shown that good-looking criminals get lighter sentences, attractive patients get more personalized health care and attractive people earn more money.

We can't change our height or the way we look without resorting to surgery. But we can all enhance our attractiveness simply by being fit, dressing well, and attending to our grooming. Even a sense of humour adds to our attractiveness.

Amazingly, some people don't seem to know the difference between proper work attire and pajamas. Their appearance influences the way they are perceived by their colleagues and superiors, yet they don't seem to get it.

If appearance and fashion aren't your strong suit, get help. It may just secure your income.

Top Ten Signs Things are OK at Work:

1. Your company is in an industry that is growing.
2. You sell superior products or services that are in high demand.
3. The company is making healthy profits.
4. The stock price is soaring.
5. Bonuses are increasing.
6. Your boss likes you.
7. Everybody else likes you.
8. You alone know how to extract candy that gets stuck in the vending machine.
9. You regularly cut your boss's lawn and wash his car.
10. You marry the founder's daughter.

Top Ten Signs the End is Nigh:

1. Your company is in an industry that is losing relevance.
2. Your products or services are not competitive.
3. What profit?
4. The stock just got de-listed.
5. Herb is your new boss.
6. Herb can't look you in the eye.
7. Nobody likes anyone.
8. The receptionist is replaced by voicemail.
9. The vending machine is gone. So is the water cooler.
10. The founder's daughter leaves you and runs away with the janitor.

PROTECT YOUR INCOME

Once you have done everything you can to secure your income you have to protect it with insurance.

The amount of insurance that you need depends on your income, expenses and debts. It should at the very least allow your family to carry on until they can reestablish themselves.

For people entering the workforce now, their greatest asset is not their car or their CD collection; it's their human capital. This is the potential income that they will earn over the course of their work life. Even someone of limited skills and acumen, with a modest income of $25,000 a year, will earn $2 million dollars of inflation-adjusted income over a career. A person's human capital is far more valuable than his automobile or home. But while people insure their cars and their homes they seldom give much thought to insuring their income.

Approximately three in 10 healthy adults will suffer a critical illness before the age of 65. A third of all stroke victims are under the age of 65. Approximately 40% of Canadians will develop some form of cancer in their lifetime. The Canadian Cancer Society estimates that two-thirds of the costs related to treatment are indirect costs not covered by provincial health plans. Yet few people purchase critical illness or disability insurance. Cost is a factor but it bears some exploration none-the-less.

Insurance is complex, and policies can be customized to a specific situation. But whatever you do, you should consult a qualified insurance professional about insuring your income. You've secured it. Now insure it.

WORK/FAMILY BALANCE

If you don't balance your career and family, you will never achieve true security. Remember, balance involves opportunity and safety. You need both, and you can't get one at the expense of the other. Canadians are learning this. Research by Millward Brown Goldfarb indicates that there has been a dramatic shift in our work/life preferences even in past 20 years. When asked in 1988 if they preferred a job with more money or more time off, 55% of respondents chose a job with more money. By 2005, almost 60% said they'd prefer a job with more time off. Job security and job satisfaction now mean more than just making money. Family obligations and community commitments matter too.

Summary

- Financial security begins with making a living.
- Choosing the right career, company, and job brings psychological and economic benefits.
- Higher education combined with work experience has the most favourable influence on increasing income.
- The brand we convey makes a lasting impression.
- Use insurance to protect your income.

VI

Pay Yourself Second

After you secure an income save a portion of it

When I started working part time as a teenager my mother would take a portion of my income, which she referred to as rent money. Unbeknownst to me, my mother had set up a savings account in my name at the bank where she worked and she diligently deposited my rent money whenever she extracted her toll from my meager paycheque. It didn't bother me, since I hardly noticed the amount. I also felt that I was helping out with the family expenses in some small way. When I graduated from university I didn't think that I had a dime to my name. Then my mother gave me back my rent money with interest. I'm a saver to this day because of my upbringing.

SAVING IS AN UNNATURAL HUMAN ACT

Once we've done everything within our power to secure an income, we have to begin to save some of it for the future. Remember, money is energy and although we have to expend much of our energy to live now, we also have to conserve some of it for later. Saving and spending are two sides to the same coin. If we don't spend all of what we earn, then we have a savings. If we spend more than we earn, then we have debt. Spend less than we earn and we'll vastly improve our probability of being financially happy. The problem is we seem to have a natural aversion to saving.

We are no longer the dedicated savers that our parents used to be. We have enjoyed a relatively lengthy period of good times, and we want to believe that they'll continue. Also, spending is a *now* thing; saving is a *later* thing. Maybe we have a primal urge to consume now like our ancestors, who never knew when or where they'd find their next meal. Our ability to see a long-term future may conflict with our instinct to consume in the shorter term. As a result, out nature may just be frustrating our nurture. This doesn't help our long-term financial security.

EASY MONEY

It will always be far easier to spend money than to make money. These days, we don't even have to leave the comfort of our home to do it. We can shop on the television or on the web. Goods come to our door by courier. We can check our bank account and transfer cash with the click of a mouse, at any time of the day or night. Swiping or clicking has desensitized us to the amount of money we part with.

In fact, we don't buy things anymore. We just make payments. We don't know what anything costs; we only know how much we pay. But it all adds up. We earn only a finite amount of income. The more we pay, the more likely it becomes that we'll take on a little debt to cover the payments. So much for saving. So much for our financial security. So much for having enough. As long as we're in debt, we'll never have enough.

IMELDA MARCOSIS

If shopping was an Olympic sport, we could all win a platinum medal. Everyone is eligible to compete, and there are no age restrictions special qualifications, certification or licenses involved. We don't even have to be particularly proficient to be successful at the game. You just need to be as productive as you possibly can, and a little bit more. We don't need much money to participate. If we don't have cash, we can use credit.

As in most sports, we can use different tactics to shop. Here are some of them:

The Just-In-Case Shopper: If we attend social functions frequently, we need a shoe for each occasion. If we play golf on different courses we need a different driver or putter for each one. In homes around the world, there are closets filled with hardly-worn clothing, almost-new shoes, and seldom-used seven irons. We can't throw them out. Who knows when we'll need them again?

The Bargain Hunter: In this strategy, we're not actually spending money when we shop, we're saving it. That's because we only buy items at a discount. If we pay \$25 for a \$40 item, we've just saved \$15. Who says saving isn't easy?

- *The Frequent Flyer:* We're not really shopping—we're collecting points. We may never redeem those points for that holiday or that toaster. But we could if we wanted to. It feels good to know that we have hundreds of thousands of points to our credit. And with each additional purchase, we accumulate more. What luxury!

- *The Self-Medicating Shopper:* When we feel a little low on happiness and self esteem we can either take a pill or go shopping. If we worry about the debt we've accumulated, we can go shopping again. There's nothing like a little retail therapy to chase the blues away.
- *The Reward Shopper:* This person justifies purchases based on some hazy logic that the item is reward for achieving some equally hazy milestone. "I haven't bitten my nails for a whole week so I'm getting a Porsche. I've been good so I deserve it, right?" If you don't think it's possible to bribe yourself—this often-employed strategy is clear proof of your naivety.
- *The Badge Collector:* This shopper must have the latest 'it' gadget or thing at the precise moment it receives

its 'it' status. If others have it—I must have it, too. Brands are used to confer a level of status and esteem which the badge collector aspires to. Generally, the level of 'badginess' is inversely proportional to the level of self-esteem of the badge collector.

- *The Defensive Shopper*: "It was the last one so I had to get it before somebody else did. Once it's gone, I can't get it anymore, so I've got to have it." The fact that it is the last one is validation enough that this is a sound purchase.
- *The Punter*: In this strategy every play is just a temporary possession. They're always looking to buy because they're always looking to sell. The difference between the buying price and the selling price don't matter so much—you win some and you lose some. Buying the item feels good, besides I can always return it for a full refund, or better yet, I can always sell it on e-Bay so there's no real downside.

Every time we go shopping without any other reason than to feel good, we jeopardize our financial security. We can all make the choice between feeling good temporarily and feeling financially secure for the rest of our lives, But it's easier said than done.

DON'T BUY THE 1,000 POUND GORILLA

While I was writing this book, I interviewed a number of people about money and what it meant in their lives. One was a former colleague who had founded the company I worked for. He sold his shares for a significant sum of money and retired. He had achieved what most of us only dream about and was happy to walk away from his business as a relatively young man with the rest of his life ahead of him.

The first question I asked him was, "What's it like when a great deal of wealth happens to you?" He leaned back in his chair and looked at the ceiling for about a minute. It felt like an eternity, but I didn't want to break his concentration—so we sat in silence. Besides, I was already somewhat used to this kind of quirkiness from him. He then leaned forward, looked at me and said, "The first thing you do when wealth happens to you is you go out and buy a 1,000-pound gorilla." Long pause. "Then you have to walk the gorilla, and you have to feed the gorilla, and you have to house the gorilla, and then you have to send it to gorilla school." Having known him for years, I knew exactly what he meant. It was his way of saying that attaining a great deal of wealth was great, but he had bought a bigger lifestyle to go with it.

Over the next few days, I pictured him walking down a road in his neighbourhood with his gorilla. Then it occurred to me that we all have our own gorilla, although it may not be as large as his. We walk down the street with our 100-pound gorilla thinking we have a pretty good gorilla until we pass someone who has a 200-pound gorilla. Then we think, "I've got to get a bigger gorilla." The more we can afford, the bigger the monkey gets. The strain of carrying the gorilla around can take its toll. And even as we go looking for a bigger one, we keep wondering how to get the monkey off our back.

LIVING THE LIFE

I once worked with a senior executive for less than a month. Within that short period, he let me know that he lived in an exclusive neighbourhood in a house decorated by a noted interior designer, drove a convertible Mercedes, and belonged to exclusive golf and fitness clubs. He apologized for arriving late to a meeting one day by informing everyone that he had been delayed as he'd dropped his children off at two separate private schools. In his own eyes, he was living *the* life.

In my experience, many people are so busy living the life that they forget how to live their own life. When status is the motivation, it slowly chips away at their personality and, after a while, all they're left with is a hollow kind of publicality. But that's what happens when we identify ourselves by our possessions.

No matter how much we accumulate, we never feel financially secure if we measure ourselves by our possessions. All we feel are scorn and envy for people who have less or more than we do.

STRETCHED

Why do we seem to have less money after we get a raise? It's because we usually buy more things.

Most of us start small, as if we have training wheels on our status symbols. But we soon graduate to the big leagues as we earn more money. The more we accumulate, the bigger the purchase and the more envy our ostentation arouses, not just in others, but in ourselves as well. No matter how much or how big or how expensive, someone else always has more than we do. You don't have to take my word for it. An American Express survey found that about half the people who make more than $200,000 feel they're just getting by. This is almost double the rate of those who make the average family income of approximately $60,000.

If we want to feel financially secure we have to aspire to see but not be seen. If we can manage our expectations we can manage our happiness. I don't mean aim low and be happy. I think you should determine the optimal level of opportunity and safety that will bring you the maximum amount of happiness. Then don't forget it.

LAY AWAKE PLAN

The average Canadian household carries about $70,000 in debt. Every Canadian has, on average, 1.5 credit cards. About half of these cards carry a balance. The average purchase with a credit card in Canada is just over $100. The debt-to-income ratio of the average Canadian household is now above 100%. The number of credit cards, the average amount purchased and the average household debt have all risen over the last 20 years by at least 50%. What's going on?

Never has so much credit been available to so many. We use the equity in our homes to secure a line of credit.

Unlike a mortgage, which gives us a chance to make up for a missed payment, a home-equity line of credit is a demand loan. Miss a payment and we might have to sell our house. There's nothing wrong with credit. It's a handy financial tool. But like a hammer or a bulldozer, it only works when we use it for its intended purpose.

As we've already discussed, its harder to save if we have to repay debt. It sounds so obvious that I hesitate even to say it: we can't save what we spend. We'll never feel financially secure if we don't have any money.

RED IS THE NEW BLACK (Debt is the new normal)

Canadians now think debt is normal. Even retired people see nothing wrong with it. An RBC Financial Group poll indicates that almost half of all Canadians do not believe it is necessary to retire debt-free. About a third of all retired Canadians have debts. This is the polar opposite to anything you would read in any financial planning textbook or hear from a financial advisor of sound mind and spirit. It is definitely not ok to retire with debt—no matter how easily we can carry it. If our perceptions of debt continue to metamorphose in this way newborns will get a slap on the bottom and a credit card.

We may think that our credit will last forever. So why save? But at the end of the day we'll discover that we've actually spent our financial security and squandered our independence.

DOWNWARD MOBILITY

In *The Millionaire Next Door* Thomas J. Stanley says the typical millionaire passes by without even drawing our attention. The distinguishing characteristics of most millionaires are that they live within their means and they're dedicated savers and investors.

If we were to write *The Bankrupt Next Door* we'd find people with similarly uniform characteristics. According to the Office of the Superintendent of Bankruptcy Canada, the typical bankrupt Canadian is a 42-year-old man with $57,000 of debt and net assets of just $500. More likely than not, he's divorced and unemployed. He doesn't save, he doesn't invest, but he thinks he can handle debt, so he keeps piling it on.

Many Canadians don't even know how much they owe. And if they discover one day that they can't meet their obligations, they don't sweat. They just go bankrupt. No one seems to care any more if they do. The number of consumer insolvencies in Canada has increased at a rate of 11.3% per year on average between 1966 and 2003. Approximately 100,000 Canadians go bankrupt each year, slightly over four cases per thousand, up from 0.15 cases per thousand in 1966. For many the primary cause is excessive consumerism. The remedy may just be a little more abstainerism.

We've become complacent about debt. Consequently, the stigma of bankruptcy has virtually disappeared.

WHAT'S YOUR FINANCIAL DROP DEAD DATE?

Approximately 20% of North Americans have no savings or cash on hand. In other words, they live paycheque to paycheque. Miss one paycheque, and there goes Johnny. Even the other 80% of us have to figure out from time to time how long we can last if the paycheques stop coming. That's our drop-dead date. It's as important as checking our blood pressure and our cholesterol count. We also have to figure out how long it would take to replace that lost income with another paycheque from a new job. That's our resurrection date. If our drop-dead date comes sooner than our resurrection date we have a problem.

How can we extend our drop-dead date? Easy. We can spend less and save more. It will act as our financial airbag when and if we have a financial crash.

FISCAL FITNESS

The savings rate in Canada represents the difference between our income and our expenditures. In 1982, Canadians saved 17 cents of every dollar they earned. Today they save less than 3 cents.

Young people starting their adult lives often spend more than they earn, but they used to do it temporarily. In 1982, 39% of Canadian households spent more money than they earned. Today 47% of them do, and in many of those households the occupants are just about to retire.

I was once asked by a doctor and his wife for advice on how they could achieve a higher degree of financial security. They were barely making their bill payments every month, and it was placing a strain on their marriage. They were making lots of money, much more than the national average. But they were spending everything they made, and more. I advised them to simply spend less than they made and start living within their means. They looked at each other, and then looked back at me, and said, "Is there another way?" There is no other way.

We need short-term savings in case our income is interrupted. This is our job security fund. We need long-term savings for retirement. We need both kinds of savings for our sense of security. We don't have to save everything we need all at once. We can start small, by cutting back on the little extras like the 500 cable channels that we never watch or the extra telephone features we don't use because we don't know how.

Once we start saving, we don't even notice it after a while.

Summary

- Saving money is crucial for financial security.
- We spend lavishly to acquire status.
- We have become complacent with debt.
- Many of us are just a couple paycheques from ruin.
- Start small and keep saving.

VII

ORDER IN THE HOUSE

The house is more than just shelter

The latest status symbol in towns and cities across the continent is not a luxury automobile; it's a dumpster in the driveway. It's ironic that something, which is associated with garbage, has replaced a Mercedes as the primary badge of privilege among polite society. Like the car, dumpsters come in all shapes, sizes and colours. Unlike the car, they convey a level of social significance within a particular neighbourhood that transcends anything a mere car can

suggest. You see a car and, you assume that it's leased and can be returned at any time. When you see the dumpster you think 'serious commitment.'

Dumpsters also have important social significance. They act as a magnet for the street and can bring a neighbourhood together faster than any block party. "Did you see the dumpster in the Smith's driveway? Let's go talk to them." People who have never even met now have something to talk about. Everyone wants to know what they are doing to the house, and what impact it may have on their property values. It seems counterintuitive, but those big rugged dumpsters generally appeal to women more than they do to men—who only see dollar signs and a poor sucker with a weak constitution. Women see great beauty in them as they chalk another one up for a lucky member of the sisterhood. The only thing the men in the neighbourhood are thinking about is how they are going to get the empty paint cans that have been sitting in their garage for years into that dumpster, without the Smith's noticing.

CURB APPEAL

We are fortunate to live in a society that recognizes property rights, and has put in place laws to protect those rights. There are many places in the world where you are little more than a squatter wherever you care to settle. Your corrugated tin shack could be taken down at any time and you would be forced to relocate. We, on the other hand, are pretty safe from these kinds of distractions.

According to Canada Housing and Mortgage Corporation about two-thirds of Canadians purchase their homes. The rest of us rent. Almost 60% of us own a single-family detached home. Another 30% own a condominium. The rest own some other form of housing.

Canadians have embraced home ownership, encouraged by strong employment prospects, low interest rates and a wide variety of payment options and lenders. More Canadians than ever can afford to buy a house. According to an RBC Financial Group report, home ownership costs such as mortgage payments, utilities, and property taxes account on average for about 35% of pre-tax income. The average goes up in large urban centers, but even there, houses remain affordable.

The average size of new homes has grown steadily as well, from 5.3 rooms in 1961 to 6.3 rooms today, and has surpassed 2,000 square feet even though the average number of household occupants has dropped from 3.0 to 2.6 over that period.

What used to be considered special or luxury features are becoming increasingly common: two-car garages, multiple bathrooms, mud rooms, central air conditioning. No wonder people spend so much time in their homes. With home theatres, built-in barbecues, hot tubs, wine cellars, indoor golf simulators, high-speed Internet connections, fully equipped home offices, and fancy kitchens, we can work, play, shop, eat and exercise without ever leaving home.

THE UPSIDEDOWN HOUSE

If you need a house and you can afford to buy one, you should just do it. Regardless of the ups and downs of the housing market, there's no time like the present to get into it. But you can protect yourself from difficulty by following a few simple tips:

- Try to spend no more than one-third of your gross household income on shelter, which includes mortgage payments, property taxes, heating and maintenance.
- If you're moving from one house to another, try to upsize in a soft market, because the discount on a more expensive property will be greater than the hit you'll take by selling your less expensive property. Likewise, try to downsize in a strong market. You'll gain

more on the sale of your more expensive property than the premium you'll pay on the less expensive property.

- If you buy a house when prices are high and rates are low then lock in the best rate you can for as long as you can. It will give you some certainty as you establish yourself.
- Buy the worst house on the best street you can afford. The other houses on the street will raise the value of yours.
- It's easier to sell a house in an urban area because the market is bigger than it is in a small town or rural setting and people appreciate amenities such as public transit, schools and hospitals. The diversified economy of a city ensures that property values won't plummet if a single company goes out of business. In a small town, you can't be so sure.

THE HOUSE IS THE BANK

A few years ago, I was presenting to a fairly large audience at a seminar in the evening. At the conclusion of the presentation there was food and drinks, and most of the audience remained. I had the opportunity to speak with a number of people that evening, but one couple, in particular, struck me because they brought their new born baby to the presentation. Although it was late in the evening they stayed until the very end. They were like a lot of young people who were just getting established in life having just purchased a house and started a family.

When I asked if they owned a house, the woman said they did, but the bank really owned it. "So you're a banker," I said. They shook their heads, but I explained that in buying a house they had gained access to the same services as they'd find in a bank: cash management, savings and investments, and credit. By owning a house, they managed their cash, followed a disciplined savings program, pursued an investment strategy and accumulated credit that they could use if they needed it. As the woman listened, she grabbed her husband's arm and said, "Honey, I'm a banker."

Just like a bank, a house contributes in many ways to our financial lives. It provides:

- *A place of security and privacy:* Like the local bank, our house provides a feeling of permanence and security.
- *A place to safeguard our assets:* Our house is the place where we keep most of our precious assets like my panini maker and the trampoline. Just ask my parents. They've kept some of my most treasured chattels in their house ever since I left home 20 years ago.

- *A means of saving:* With each mortgage payment you make, you get closer to your goal of home ownership while saving a portion of your income. And it happens like clockwork, every month, even as we sleep. Financial plans don't come any better than that.
- *A long-term investment:* With each mortgage payment, we build our equity, just like an investment in a GIC at a bank. When we renovate the kitchen we also make an investment. Updating the bathroom is an investment too. In most parts of the country, residential real estate has proven to be a good investment and a hedge against inflation because of its low correlation with many other financial assets. And, since home ownership is typically a long-term proposition, it makes us patient and conservative investors, the best kind to be.
- *A source of credit:* A home equity loan is like a mortgage but with a shorter term and a fixed rate. A home equity line of credit is a revolving loan that you can use at any time, with a floating rate of interest. Your house gives you access to both.

STEALING HOME

Having discussed the benefits of owning a house, let's talk for a moment about protecting those benefits.

Homeowners insure their houses and the contents against occurrences like flooding and fire. In fact, most mortgage lenders insist on it. But many people don't take the time to ensure that their policy is up to date or that the coverage is sufficient. Each year the cost of materials from lumber to light bulbs—goes up, not to mention the cost of labour. So next time the renewal notice arrives, read it.

In the event of death, illness or job loss, how would you or your family make the mortgage payments? Most lenders offer creditor insurance that covers these payments if you get sick, lose your job or die. Alternatively, critical-illness, disability and term life insurance, as we discussed earlier, will do the same job.

THE BANK BALANCE

We're much more likely to stick with a mortgage than a retirement plan. That's not a bad thing. A house gives us a vehicle to build wealth and develop the habit of saving a significant portion of our income. We also achieve a higher degree of security from a physical asset than we do from a financial asset, which seems more temporary.

That explains why two-thirds of Canadian household members own their own home, while fewer than one-third own stocks. As time passes, you should try to balance the equity in your home with the value of your long-term savings or retirement assets. At the time of retirement you will have a diversified source of income worth a significant amount. For example, the average Canadian household with an annual income of $60,000 could retire comfortably with real estate wealth of $250,000 and financial wealth of $250,000. With government support payments, these assets will deliver a reasonably secure retirement.

FALL BACK ON

A house is the most expensive purchase most of us will ever make in our lives. Until we pay it off, it's usually the biggest expense we'll ever have to cover. Our house provides a place to raise our children and the nest that they can return to after they leave home. It's also our link to neighbours, friends and community. It gives us a great sense of financial and emotional comfort and security. And that's what this book is all about.

Summary

- A house is your biggest purchase, and one of your greatest securities.

- Begin putting money away for a house as soon as you secure your income.
- Buy a house when you need one.
- Buy what you can afford, you can always move up later.
- Try to balance the value of the equity in your home with the value of your other investments.

VIII

FROM RETIREMENT TO EXPIREMENT

Why long-term savings and planning for the future are crucial for security

Canadians generally regard retirement as an afterthought. They think retirement is for old people, and they don't begin planning for it until later in life. We all like to think we're young, and we try to live in the moment. Thinking about our long-term future takes us out of the moment and makes us feel old. Gradually, though, our bodies start to make creaking noises, we need glasses to read, our vocabulary includes more Latin medical terms, and it takes us much longer to get over viruses and cocktail parties. Around the time when we reach fifty, we start to take retirement more seriously.

Many of us dream of retiring early but know we can't afford it. According to a study by Desjardins Financial, 80% of Canadians feel optimistic that their retirement dreams are achievable. However, only 44% of currently retired Canadians say that they're actually living their retirement dream. For most Canadians, retirement expectations will exceed their experience.

We already know that a continuous and dependable stream of income for life will provide us with a sense of financial security. We know too that we need to secure an income and save a portion for later to deliver this dependable income when we retire. Now we need to develop a realistic expectation of what we want to do in retirement and the amount of money it will take to do it.

START SMOKING

In the heady days of the stock market, back in the 1990s, I had the dubious pleasure of meeting a middle-aged man who wanted to invest in a high-performing Tech Fund.

He had seen an ad boasting of big returns, and he wanted to get some.

I discovered that he had not saved much money, nor was he particularly interested in saving. But he intended to retire early and travel the world. Clearly, there was a large gap between what he wanted to do, when he wanted to do it, and what he was prepared to do to achieve it. Hence, his interest in the go-go tech fund du jour.

At the end of our discussion, as he looked to me for a response, I leaned forward and said in a very serious tone, "My advice to you, sir, is to start smoking".

During the silence that ensued, I felt like adding, "You might try a diet of chicken tartar and cut the seatbelts out of your car, as well." Then I showed him why he could not possibly attain his retirement dream on his current financial trajectory. I never heard from him again. But there are lots more Canadians just like him.

By timing their death in a more fiscally prudent way, these Canadians can feel more confident that they won't outlive their retirement assets.

Having a retirement plan is not the same as retirement planning, which involves taking a hard look at what we want to do, when we want to do it, and how much it will take to fund it. We usually have a clearer idea of these factors when we reach our 40s and 50s. At that stage of our lives, it's high time to prepare a formal plan to achieve our retirement dream.

RETIREMENT WAS A PERIOD OF POVERTY

The idea of retirement as a period of leisure and freedom to indulge personal interests is a relatively recent development. Up until the first half of the last century, retirement was a period of poverty for the vast majority of people who lived long enough to experience it. Generally, people worked until they died or for as long as they were physically able. When they could no longer work their family took them in. There really was not much opportunity to accumulate an adequate savings.

Canada introduced social security in 1927 with the Old Age Pensions Act. The program was meant to protect elderly Canadians from extreme poverty. Eligibility was limited to British subjects aged 70 or older who had lived in Canada for 20 years. Only seniors who earned less than

$365 per year including pension benefits could qualify for the princely sum of $20 a month. Although the eligibility age was 70, the average life expectancy for Canadians was only 59.

Things have improved since then for Canadians facing retirement. Old Age Security (OAS) was introduced in 1952, the Canada Pension Plan/Quebec Pension Plan (CPP/QPP), in 1965, and the Guaranteed Income Supplement (GIS) in 1967. Canadians now enjoy more security during the increasingly lengthy final period of their lives. But few of us know exactly how much we can expect from public retirement programs, and many of us believe these plans are much more generous than they actually are.

CPP/QPP, OAS and GIS are meant to supplement our personal retirement savings, not to support a lifestyle of leisure or privilege. For that we need either an employer-sponsored pension plan or an individual plan like an RRSP, or both.

If you are covered by an employer-sponsored defined benefit pension plan you are fortunate. If your plan is indexed to inflation you are truly fortunate. Unfortunately, the number of employees who are covered by these plans is declining. Employers with defined benefit pension plans view them as an expensive burden. Many companies have converted their defined benefit plans to defined contribution plans, passing the risk of earning an inadequate return on to the employee. Being typical Canadians who don't pay much attention to their finances, most employees are ill equipped to manage this risk effectively.

The unlucky 60% of Canadian employees who are not covered by an employer-sponsored pension plan have to rely heavily on their own private retirement savings plans, primarily the RRSP. The government thinks we should save 18% of our earned income for retirement. That's where it sets the limit on eligible contributions. Whether we agree or not, we should make this contribution every year. In our old age, we'll thank ourselves for doing it.

I'M AFRAID OF GETTING OLD AND BEING BROKE

As Canadians live longer than ever, we have more time to spend in retirement, if we plan properly. Thirty years ago the average Canadian retired at 65 and might expect to live another 10 years. The current retirement age for many of us has declined to 61 years, but the average 65-year-old can now expect to live another 20 to 30 years. Assuming we enter the workforce at age 20; the ratio of work years to retired years in Canada has declined from approximately 6:1 to 2.5:1 in just the past thirty years. This means that our margin for error has shrunk dramatically.

To ensure you do not outlive your money you will have to be much more diligent about retirement planning. We may want to live to a ripe old age, but not if we're eating cat food and living in a car.

SCRAMBLED EGGS

The whole point of saving for retirement is to create a nest egg large enough to produce a satisfactory income that will support you for the rest of your life. For the average person of modest resources, this will mean living off some portion of income and principal. However, the farther we are from retirement the harder it is to estimate how much we'll need. So most of us don't even bother. A recent poll by RBC Financial Group determined that only 31% of Canadians have actually figured out how much money they will need to retire comfortably.

It makes sense that the proportion of annual income we save should roughly correspond to the number of retirement years we think we'll enjoy relative to our work years. For example, if we think we'll work 45 years and retire for 15, a ratio of 3:1, then we should save about a third of our income over the course of our work life.

This will be difficult in the early years and easier in the pre-retirement years. Barring this you may consider working longer. You want to hit retirement with enough velocity to create a financial trajectory that is capable of carrying you well into old age. The only thing you want stopping your trajectory is your death. Otherwise, it means you ran out of money, in which case you may just wish you were dead.

Most investment companies and financial pundits recommend that we save enough money for retirement to generate 70% of our pre-retirement income. To me, this does not make a lot of sense. For one thing, our final income is usually at or near its peak while our expenses are at a low point especially if we've paid off the mortgage and put the kids through school. In fact, the years leading up to retirement usually provide the most disposable income, as our earnings increase and our expenses diminish. These are the power saving years. We require much less of our pre-retirement income to support our customary lifestyle. As I mentioned earlier, we should have little or no debt when we reach retirement.

The proper way to calculate the size of the nest egg we'll require is to start with the outcome we want and work backward. Once we know what we want to do in retirement we can figure out how much it will cost. Do we want to fly six times a year to the Bahamas or just stay at home and watch baseball? Read good books or drive fast cars? Once we figure out what we want to do, we can then calculate how much money we'll need to cover our retirement costs and the size of the nest egg we'll need to provide the income.

According to Professor Moshe Milevski of York University, we can achieve a 99% probability that we won't outlive our retirement assets with a nest egg of approximately 30 times the amount of our first-year retirement expenses. For example, someone who has first-year retirement expenses of $30,000 needs a $900,000 pre-tax nest egg to feel 99% certain that he won't outlive his money. The required amount we have to save goes down depending on the income we get from government and employer-sponsored retirement programs. This sounds like a lot of money to the average Canadian, but we're talking about a virtual certainty of not experiencing retirement ruin.

Many personal finance books suggest that we withdraw money from our retirement savings at a fixed rate of between 3% and 5%. I think we should determine the amount, not the rate, of our withdrawals. That's because most of us will need to deplete our principal as we age.

As this happens, we'll inevitably have to start withdrawing a higher proportion of our nest egg every year.

HOW TO BLOW YOUR RETIREMENT (Don't Save Enough)

As we discussed earlier, the government tries to encourage Canadians to save for their retirement by allowing us to contribute 18% of earned income to an RRSP. Most of us don't come close to contributing our allowable limit. Approximately 75% of tax filers are eligible to make RRSP contributions, but only 31% actually make them. The average contribution is about $2,500 per year, meaning that most of us make a contribution that's much less than the government allows.

The lower our income, the less we save. That's partly because the tax deduction doesn't provide as much incentive to a low-income earner as it does to a higher-income earner. So the people who take the most advantage of the RRSP program are the people who are already in pretty good financial shape.

Even after Canadians contribute to an RRSP, we often withdraw the money early for non-retirement purposes. The RRSP has become an emergency source of funds for a lot of Canadians. Many are using it to pay bills and take vacations. This is a big mistake. Once the money is removed, it is taxed as income, and the contribution room is lost forever.

INVESTOR THEOLOGY (Don't Have a Plan)

To save and invest properly for retirement and financial security, we need a plan. Plans are especially important when we don't feel comfortable with something. Most of us don't feel comfortable with saving and investing money. A plan helps.

Really good plans provide perspective. They tell us where we are, where we're going, and how to get there. The best plans take into account unforeseen events. If you can anticipate adverse outcomes, you can mitigate risk and increase the likelihood of achieving your desired outcome.

Most Canadians do not have a written financial plan. Fewer still have a plan prepared by a financial professional. For too many Canadians financial security is a matter of blind faith. That makes for bad investing. Faith without a plan leads to irrational behaviour. When we believe in something, in spite of the facts, then we're practicing investor theology. Since investing is much more difficult than just saving, we all need a plan.

FINANCIAL PROMISCUITY (Don't Follow Your Plan)

In finance as in other aspects of life, the 80/20 rule applies: 80% of us don't know what we're doing, 20% do. The problem is that most people think they are part of the 20%, who actually understand financial planning. Unfortunately, ignorance comes with a high economic and emotional cost.

Having spoken with thousands of investors during my time at a large direct mutual fund company, I can't tell you how many times I've witnessed investors being swayed by emotion. People with seven good funds, for example, and one not so good fund suddenly start shifting things around, usually at the wrong time. They begin to lose perspective. After a while, they're off their plan. They no longer own a portfolio of investments, just a collection of formerly good ideas.

A little bit of information and a lot of choice can be lethal to the retail investor's financial security. Studies have shown that investors often underperform when they enjoy more choice. Without the discipline to stick with a simple plan, they end up performing financial self-mutilation.

After twenty-plus years and thousands of conversations with people about their investments, I can honestly say that most of them would have been better off in a diversified balanced fund. Although that doesn't mean we should all just plunk our money down and forget about it.

HOW MUCH PAIN CAN YOU HANDLE?

The average investor is now much less concerned with absolute returns and much more concerned with preserving capital. Most of us want to manage the growing perceived risk in our lives and minimize the surprises. Hence the trend toward packaged solutions: wrap programs, lifecycle portfolios or managed portfolios. In these portfolios the investment manager creates a diversified suite of portfolios from a group of funds. Each portfolio is managed according to a particular risk quotient. In the case of lifecycle portfolios, they gradually become more conservative as retirement approaches. These products offer a great deal of comfort because they emphasize risk management rather than absolute performance. But it's not always easy matching portfolios with people's comfort zones.

While I was chair of a product development committee, I had the opportunity to launch a suite of managed portfolios. These are comprehensive portfolios of mutual funds that are managed according to a given level of risk. In order to assess their risk tolerance, clients self-selected their appropriate portfolio by completing a profile questionnaire. Most people who completed the questionnaire properly turned out to be risk averse and were directed to a portfolio with an income bias. In other words, their investment may not have a great chance of leaping higher in value, but it would not likely lose its original value. But there was evidence that many clients had modified their answers to reposition themselves further up the risk spectrum, at their own peril.

When it comes to our investments none of us likes to think of ourselves as a 98-pound weakling. Yet most people can't handle as much risk as they think they can. It's essential when we make a plan for our future financial security that we understand what we want to achieve and how much risk we can tolerate as we do it. Otherwise, we will inevitably fail.

As research shows, the average person feels the pain of an investment loss much more acutely than the pleasure of an investment gain. This means that investors will react to losses more strongly than they react to gains. As risk increases in a portfolio, the chances of a loss increase as well. Investors who react inappropriately will likely suffer further losses. Better to get the right amount of opportunity and safety.

WE USED TO INVEST TO BEAT INFLATION

Recently, I was dealing with a cabinet maker who did some work on my office. After we dispensed with our business, he began asking me questions about our company and what we did. He told me he had an investment portfolio, but he didn't think he was getting anywhere, and didn't know if his advisor was being effective. I asked him what he meant. He replied, "It doesn't seem to do much". When I pressed him about his expectations, he simply said that he thought it would go up more. At the time we spoke inflation was under 2% and the markets were very benign. I told him that we used to invest to beat inflation and that his portfolio might just be fine since inflation was near historical lows. It became clear to me that, although his advisor may be doing a fine job with his portfolio, he was not doing a great job of informing his clients of what to expect.

Before the bull market in the 1990s, investors knew they had to put money away every year and aim to beat inflation. They understood that the further we move away from inflation protection and the bigger returns we expect, the more risk we take on.

These days, most people don't even know what inflation is. We spend so much that we don't put any money away, so inflation doesn't really matter to us. By the time we do start saving, we don't just need to beat inflation; we also need big returns, which only come, if we're lucky, if we take big risks.

Even people who have the right portfolio for their circumstances may have an advisor who doesn't explain how the market works; that big swings in value cause discomfort, for example, or that a portfolio that doesn't do much may be exactly what most people need. There's nothing wrong with stability, consistency, and predictability. They all add up to sustainability, and who doesn't want that.

The key to achieving a retirement plan is to put money away every day, week, month or year. Getting the money into the plan is more important than what happens to it once it's in there.

TIME IS MONEY

I like to think of retirement saving as similar to building your personal leisure company. The sole business objective of the company is to secure your future relaxation and enjoyment. While you are working, you go along putting money into your company and growing its assets responsibly. Once you retire, the company becomes active and begins paying you a salary. The only thing you have to do to earn the paycheque is tend to the garden, read a book, golf or travel.

There are really three reliable ways in which to ensure that you do not run out of money before you run out of life; start earlier, work longer and save more. After the experience of the 1990s, most people have eliminated cranking up portfolio risk/return as a dependable option.

If we all began socking money away for the future when we start working, we wouldn't have to worry about retirement planning nearly as much later in life.

THE OPPOSITE OF LIFE INSURANCE

Earlier we talked about life insurance to protect our income and provide for our family in case we die too soon.

If we die our beneficiaries will receive a lump-sum death benefit. In retirement we have the opposite problem. We may live too long and run out of money. A great way to hedge our risk of living too long is to purchase a life annuity. This is an insurance contract that is the opposite of life insurance: we pay a lump sum to an insurance company, which then pays us a fixed sum every month for the remainder of our lives. We are betting we'll live a long life while the company is betting we won't.

If the insurance company is correct, and we die sooner, then the company makes no more payments. Different types of annuities work in different ways. There are term-certain annuities, for example, that guarantee payments to our beneficiary for a fixed period regardless of when we die, but the payments are lower than those for a regular annuity. There are also variable annuities whose value fluctuates with the market, but these are more expensive. The problem with most annuities is that there is no flexibility in the payments and the general level of interest rates at the time of purchase determines those payments. The payments are also fixed and don't typically take into account inflation, which becomes more significant the longer we live.

Splitting the nest egg between some portion of investments and insurance will become increasingly popular as more people live longer. In the investment portion of our portfolio, we have the flexibility and liquidity to do as we choose, but in the insurance portion, we give up our flexibility for the certainty of an income for life regardless of how long we live. In general, putting one-third of your assets into an annuity and keeping control over the other two-thirds might be the best course for those who are worried about longevity.

Regardless of how you slice the egg, you should diversify the sources of your retirement income so you don't have to depend on any single source.

SHADES OF GRAY

According to Statistics Canada 22% of retirees returned to paid employment after their initial retirement. This was more prevalent among Canadians who left the workplace prior to the age of 60, those who worked in a professional occupation, or were in good health. These people have the most attractive employment and income opportunities, which again, confirm the value of an education and a portfolio of relevant skills. The primary reasons for leaving work were job dissatisfaction and the perception of failing health. The number-one reason for re-entering the workforce was financial, and almost half returned on a part-time basis. As we come to terms with greater longevity retirement futurists believe that this trend will accelerate.

Many of us do not want to retire or do not believe we'll have enough money to retire at age 65. Some of us would like to remain engaged but simply reduce our work commitment. This will require an adjustment to the public and private pension system to better reflect this new dynamic. Many pension plans base their benefits on a formula involving the final year's earnings, which does not encourage an individual to ease into retirement. Nor does the public system offer much flexibility for someone who wants to take this route. It actually penalizes us for working past retirement age in the form of claw-backs and a reduced benefit period. Each system needs to accommodate people who want to reduce their work commitment gradually.

What we think of as retirement is clearly very different from the retirement that Canadians experienced in the first half of the last century. If they were fortunate enough to live that long it was not a very significant or very pleasurable period in the average person's life. The word "retirement" is really a reference to having withdrawn from paid work. As such, it's more reflective of a moment in time than a significant period of your life. It certainly does not suggest a time of relaxation—unless you're talking about the ultimate relaxation: death. The length and meaning of this increasingly important period of the average Canadian's life now deserves to have a name that more accurately reflects the nuance of our aspirations.

Some already have their own name for this period. For many it's called: consulting or freelancing. At the top echelon of the business world it's called Chairman. Others just say they are a private investor, but these different terms unintentionally confuse the issue. What we really need is a universally accepted name for the "Retirement to Experiment" period of life. Here are a few I thought of, but dismissed for various reasons:

- *Relaxment:* not for everyone; just the shuffle board set
- *Pastimement:* too pedestrian; I'm picturing senior mall rats
- *Pleastment:* sounds nice; but assumes working was miserable
- *Rewardment:* not bad; suggests you earned it
- *Slothment:* nahhh
- *Blissment:* spiritual; but a little too fou fou for some
- *Kissmybuttment:* too strong

If work life is characterized as a period where we look after our needs and, post-work life as a period where we look after our wants, then "Desirement" could be a good handle to replace retirement. It makes sense; we want this period to be an expression of a life that we could achieve if we enjoyed financial independence. When someone asks you what you're up to, you can smugly reply, that you are "Desired". It sounds kind of funny now, but with more use it will take its rightful place in our consciousness. Unfortunately, most Canadians are woefully unprepared for a transition to the final stage in their life. If they don't get serious about planning and don't accumulate a satisfactory nest egg it will still be just a retirement.

Summary

- Many Canadians have unrealistic expectations about retirement
- Retirement is a relatively new concept.
- Most people are afraid of running out of money, but have not taken the time to determine how much money they'll need.
- Many don't have a formal written plan.
- Many who do have a plan, don't stick to it.
- The real secret to retirement is to start thinking about it and saving for it early.
- Getting money into the plan is more important than how much it makes once it's there.

IX

COMFORT NOW

You need to see the future so that you can live in the moment

After thousands of real conversations with real people in the real world, I've found that financial security and peace-of-mind for most people is actually nothing more than the realization that they'll make it. That they are going to be OK.

Every financial decision we make in life has consequences: the early decisions, because their effects compound over the course of a lifetime; the later decisions, because there is less margin for error as time passes. This means every year we age, the financial and emotional stakes rise higher.

We now know that being prepared is essential for financial security. Unfortunately, most Canadians don't know where to go or whom to turn to get their financial show on the road.

A DRUNK IN THE DESERT

Some people believe that when you are born your life is already written somewhere. Others believe that life is what you make it. Who is right? I think it's a little bit of both. You can't choose your parents or the circumstances you are born into. You learn certain values and beliefs by virtue of the experiences you have as an infant and, later a child, a teen, and a young adult. After that, it's pretty much up to you what you want to do with your life.

Some of us prefer to leave life's outcomes to fate. Others live in the past. Some live in hope of a better life where they see themselves as happier and more fulfilled.

In my opinion, the only way to truly experience the most that life has to offer is to live in the moment. But we've discovered we cannot live in the moment unless we have an easy mind, and we cannot have an easy mind if we do not feel secure about the future. The first step to living in the moment is to take stock of how we deal with money. Almost everyone is afraid of running out of money. As for regrets, many wish they had taken a greater interest in their finances along the way. Most of us wish we'd started saving earlier, and realize that we need help.

YOU CAN'T TICKLE YOURSELF

There are lots of pleasurable things you can do to yourself, but tickling isn't one of them. Somebody else has to do it for you.

So why can't you tickle yourself? Studies have shown that you cannot tickle yourself because there needs to be some incongruity or tension present in the situation. Believe it or not, your laughter is actually a form of panic because you're not quite sure what to expect. When you try to tickle yourself you're in complete control of the situation. Even if

you touch yourself in the same places and in the same manner as your tickler, you will not have the same reaction. No tension—no laughter.

So what does this have to do with money? Well most people are funny about their money. Not funny: 'Ha Ha', but funny peculiar. Largely, it's because they lack perspective.

Just as our brain prevents us from tickling ourselves, it also prevents most of us from making financial decisions that contribute to or maximize our happiness. Our brain is trained to filter out the things that we do. For example, when we are conscious of our breathing it becomes labored or unnatural. It returns to normal when we stop thinking about it.

Why don't we turn to other people for financial advice? Just as tickling has to involve a tickler and a ticklee, good financial health should involve an advisor and advisee. Whether or not the other person is a professional, it's a good idea to get a different perspective on our finances.

DON'T BE A "C" CLIENT

Most financial advisors and companies classify clients in three segments according to the actual or potential revenues they realize from us. Depending on the metrics they use, each of us is generally classified as an "A", "B" or "C" client. The "C" clients are the ones who do not generate much revenue; hence they don't get much attention. The "B" clients generate good revenue and help to pay the rent. At the top of the food chain are the "A" clients. They are the whales who receive most of the attention. Financial advisors strive to keep the "A" clients happy while trying to turn the promising "B" clients into "A" clients. They'd prefer to jettison the "C" clients as soon as they attract enough "A" and "B" clients.

You know you're a "C" client when:

- Nobody calls you.
- Every communication you get is a form letter.
- You don't get invited to the client-appreciation wine and cheese parties.
- When you call, you only get to speak to your advisor's assistant.
- Your advisor goes on vacation and doesn't tell you.
- Your advisor doesn't remember your name.

At all costs try to avoid being somebody's "C" client. There's somebody out there to whom you're an "A" client. Find them.

DON'T GET ADVICE—GET HELP

The greatest value we receive from professionals is not their knowledge, but their perspective.

These days most financial services executives tell you that they stand for "Wealth accumulation, Wealth management and Wealth preservation". The industry takes a very left-brain, rational approach to products and services while the consumer is very right brain focused.

Industry provides	Consumer says
Best of Breed Products	"Nobody calls me"
Advice	"I need help"
Planning Tools	"Just tell me if I'm going to make it"

Today most of us ignore financial services advertising. They have problems that need real solutions, not just financial products and services. Advisors sell products people want. Helpers apply solutions to people's problems.

We read our insurance policy after the flood, and we buy alarm systems after the break-in. That's what I did! After the bear market ravaged our savings in the 1990s, we began to realize we needed financial help as well. Taking control of our finances doesn't mean we have to do it all ourselves. If we don't enjoy something or we're not good at it or we're frightened by it we probably won't do it, at least not very well. So why not pay someone to do it?

GET TO THE PART WHERE MY TEETH GET WHITER

When you're managing people's money you are a financial advisor. When you're managing people's money and emotions you are a Financial Therapist. I've always thought of myself as the latter. I want to help people gain a better understanding of their feelings toward money. On an economic level I'm facilitating some specific financial objective, but on an emotional level I'm really selling financial security and peace of mind.

An Advisor is a good talker, but a Therapist is a good listener. If I'm going to be effective, I like to know about and sometimes get involved in every financial decision a client faces. This includes everything from buying a car to buying a house. Just like a real therapist I don't impose my views and attitudes on clients. Good financial therapy should not be preachy or pedantic. It should be collaborative. We do it together.

If you have a Financial Advisor and you're not happy because you don't know where you stand, you never hear from him or only once a year, you don't like or trust him, or you don't feel comfortable asking questions, then your advisor's not really helping you. But don't just get a new advisor, get a helper.

At the end of the day, the only thing I, or any financial advisor, have to sell is perspective. There really is no value to simply being a purveyor of financial products. When your university and grocery store want to sell you financial services products—they have become a commodity.

Lots of guides suggest what to look for in a financial advisor. They talk about the usual stuff like trustworthiness, credentials and experience. The trick is to find someone who you like, who can communicate without jargon; someone who helps you to understand where you are and where you're going.

Too many people can't see the forest for the trees. They are concerned with things that don't really matter, such as; daily, weekly or monthly returns or, whether or not, one product costs slightly more than the other. The only thing that matters is whether or not you are on track to achieve your outcome—whatever that may be. The prize is not financial, but emotional: knowing that you have enough to be financially secure. That you will achieve financial independence. That you're going to be OK.

PUSH THE ROCK

When you tell people you are writing a personal finance book it's surprising how many ask, "Do you really think you can get someone who's a financial basket case to change their ways?" I generally tell them "No." But if I could get them to think about and, perhaps, better understand their views, attitudes and habits toward money, investing and financial securities—then I've helped. I'd be happy if I can just push the rock a little bit further. If nothing else, I hope to promote a more enlightened attitude toward money—one that's not just hung up on wealth.

Everyone wants an easy path to wealth, but they don't want to have to do the heavy lifting. "Just write me a prescription and we'll get the show on the road." As a result, there are plenty of books out there, which promise you wealth if you only follow a few simple, rules, steps, habits or lessons. They all fill you with hope and you resolve to change the way you live your life. You're energized for a while, then one day, you look in the mirror—the cape and tights are gone, and you're just you again.

I'm not promising to transform your life overnight. Change is unsettling. Good change, bad change, it doesn't matter; it's all unsettling. That's because we are human. We are organic creatures who are flawed and ruled largely by emotion. We are far less rational than we think we are. Our instincts don't help us much with complex adaptive systems. But in order to change, you have to determine what specific things you are going to do differently today than you did yesterday.

While we are changing, life is changing ever more quickly all the time. As the pace of change accelerates there will be more opportunity, which means potentially more vulnerability. I believe we all have an optimal level of prospect and refuge, which will generate the maximum level of prosperity and happiness for us. The odds are that no matter how bad things are we always find a way to get by. We will always find ways to cope and take care of our primary needs. It's a survival instinct we all have which we don't even have to invoke—it just kicks in automatically. But our goal is financial security and an easy mind so merely coping just won't do. There is a right path or financial trajectory for each of us. We just have to find it.

Life is short. It just doesn't seem like it now. We don't think of multiples of years as a short period of time until we reflect. We tend to think we can put things off because there is lots of time. But the truth is…it goes quickly.

So, right about now, you may be asking yourself "Am I going to be OK?" Well, that all depends. It depends on whether you take the time to see your future and prepare for it. The emotional stakes are too high to get it wrong. If you're having trouble—get help.

Summary

- If we know we're going to be okay later, we will have comfort now.
- The only way we can have comfort now is by envisioning the future we desire and acting accordingly.
- Most of us do not have the time, resources, expertise, or inclination to maximize our financial planning on our own.
- The best strategy is to get help.
- Start today, not tomorrow.

SHAMELESS LAST WORDS

Writing this book has caused me to question my own views and attitudes toward money. I was desperate to get out of a job that paid very well. I took up yoga. I read a book about meditation. I was really searching for some perspective myself. I don't pretend that I have put money in a perspective that gives me peace-of-mind every single day of my life. But I do believe I have put money in a better place.

It has been a kind of psychological self-analysis for me. I didn't do it alone, though. I had the input of many amateur therapists with whom I spoke along the way.

I treated every conversation like a wonderful accident. Like the hand of fate brought them to me at precisely the moment that I needed perspective about something. Each added clarity to the picture in some way. I guess I really just wanted to know if I was going to be OK.

While I was writing this book the tone and approach changed slightly. I was originally writing for people who were somewhat aware of money and had a sense of what role it played in their lives. But along the way I met many people who not only knew nothing about money, they also didn't seem to care. Although they were blissfully ignorant, I couldn't help but notice the train on the horizon that was on the very track where they were standing. I wanted to explore the reasons why we may not be adept at handling money and, present a simple process for achieving financial security that I have seen work in the real world. My goal was to make you think rather than just tell you what to do.

We all know that money isn't everything. However, it's a heck of a lot of things. Some of the most important things it can represent are choice, freedom and independence. I think it's essential that every one of us make a conscious decision to learn about money and to see our financial future. There is a right path. It may take you to some strange places, but it is your path. Your milestones will act as the footprints and breadcrumbs of your journey. They will mark your successes. Along the way you will make mistakes. Don't let your mistakes go to waste. Learn from them. You have to face your fears and try to conquer them. Learn from the wisdom of others. Some day when you look back and connect all the dots of your life hopefully you will have earned the outcome you desired.

I welcome your comments and would enjoy hearing about your personal experiences. Please feel free to contact me at francis@amigoingtobeok.com .

Afterthought

A MONETARY LAPSE OF REASON

False Gods and financial myths

We all like to think we make financial decisions that contribute to, or even maximize our happiness. Unfortunately, we do not always do this. Classical economists will have you believe that people are rational beings who happily go along in life efficiently governed by logic and common sense. But as you already know: we are far from perfect and don't always make decisions that deliver optimal satisfaction. Too often, we seem to be ruled equally by emotion and superstition, with fleeting bouts of reason. Essentially we're human.

Many of us are governed by certain money beliefs. I liken some of these money beliefs to urban legends. You know the stories about alligators in the sewers, or the friend of a friend of a friend who hears about someone who went on a trip to another city, was drugged, and woke up missing a kidney. Or maybe it was the friend of a friend who went to a wedding where the groom finds out about a fling between his bride and his best man after the ceremony—just prior to the reception. There is no evidence to suggest any of these fantastic stories are actually true, yet we cringe and believe them and ask for more lurid details. We even do our part by propagating the stories, only now it has happened to a friend of our friend's friend elevating the tales from incredulous to our inner gossip mill.

Like urban legends, our money beliefs are passed from person to person as absolute truths. They are usually passed to us by a person of trust such as a parent, relative, mentor or friend. The beliefs may be modified and adjusted for the times, but they are all underpinned by some common or archetypal fear we collectively share. The focal point generally being: we will not have enough money to feel secure.

Whether we firmly believe them or simply entertain the notion, our money beliefs can often have a detrimental effect on our long-term sense of financial security. The money beliefs and myths presented here are in no particular order. They are based on real conversations that I have had with many people over the years.

Belief No. 1:

I'll be Ahead if I Just Keep Putting Money in a GIC

Why do we put money away? We do it for the simple fact that we likely don't need it now and want to use it later, or we are creating a buffer to meet significant, unexpected expenses or income shortfalls. The problem with using it later is; every day, month and year that goes by will see the purchasing power of that money shrink due to inflation. In the days before banks and the financial services industry had gained broad acceptance it was suitable to hide money that we saved in a jar, or stuff it under the mattress. Aside from being a terribly unsafe way to squirrel away hard earned money—it was not a very viable means to keep up with escalating prices. There had to be a more efficient way to sock money away for the future.

Since those stash and bury days, the financial services industry has become much more popular. Many of us have had a relationship with financial institutions from the time we were children. We have access to one of the strongest, most vibrant banking and financial services categories in the world. We tend to look to them to satisfy most of our financial needs. For many of us—our first introduction to investing was through a guaranteed investment certificate (GIC). We commit some minimum amount of money for a specified term of up to 5 years. In return we are guaranteed a certain amount of interest on our principal. GICs pay a higher rate of interest than a regular savings account because they are not liquid until they mature, but their primary popularity is their convenience and safety.

LAZY MONEY GETS HIT WITH THE FAT TAX

The government appears to have an unwritten policy, whereby; it will tax the laziest and most conservative investments at the maximum rate while giving a break to the more creative and riskier investments. Capitals gains and, to a lesser extent, dividends are more favourably taxed than interest income, which is taxed the same as employment income. GICs produce interest income and this normally means you will get to keep a lower portion of your returns than on other types of investments—regardless of your marginal tax rate (the rate of tax on the last dollar of earnings).

If you hold GICs outside of a tax-sheltered plan like an RRSP the combined effect of inflation and taxes may be damaging to your financial health. In 2004, Professor Moshe Milevski of York University looked at the real after-tax (RAT) return of GICs over the long term to see what effect taxes and inflation had on these investments. They concluded that the strategy of rolling 1-year GICs during the last 30 years would have produced a negative RAT for any Canadian whose marginal tax rate exceeded 35.5%, which currently equates to approximately $70,000 of annual income. The results were not materially different for longer term 3 and 5 year GICs that typically pays a higher rate of interest.

Saving and investing is all about time and place. The longer your investment time horizon, say anything over

5 years, the more resourceful the place you should put your money because it will likely generate a higher return with more favourable tax treatment. Unless you are completely risk averse or have a very low marginal tax rate, it can be a mistake to treat taxable savings vehicles as long-term investments. As Professor Milevski's paper stated "the strategy of rolling over so-called risk-free GICs outside a tax shelter is a sure way to destroy long-term wealth."

Belief No. 2:

My House is My Retirement

The thing that stuck with me most when my wife and I bought our first house in the early '90s was the amount of people who seemed to be house poor. It was early in a recession that affected Canada more deeply and longer than most countries. House prices had dropped about 25% form their peak. They were referring to it as a "housing bust". And it caught a lot of first time homebuyers off guard. Many never dreamed they would see the value of their house depreciate so much, so fast. I'll never forget the houses we toured which had outdoor resin garden furniture as a dining room set. House prices have since surpassed their former highs. But the experience was a stark reminder to my wife and me of the need to be diversified with our assets.

HOUSE POOR FOR SURE

You can now buy houses with as little as 5% down. At the time of writing they were proposing no money down. These days the average person who buys a house no longer thinks about how much house they can afford. They think, "How much can I carry?" And with interest rates near historical lows they can carry a lot. Perhaps more than they should. When you're committing less money up front you tend to be less diligent in determining how much you can really afford. Everything looks affordable when you only have to put 5% down.

The trend in the overheated U.S. markets is the interest only mortgage, which by 2005 represented about 70% of the new mortgages issued. They are what the name suggests; no portion of the principle is paid down, only the interest on the mortgage. It sounds like renting to me, but with all of the liability of home ownership. We don't buy a house anymore, we buy a payment, and that payment is highly levered to the rate of interest.

The house as retirement strategy is a highly undiversified strategy for retirement. It was largely created by the equity market meltdown that we suffered through in the early part of the millennium and emblematic of the cyclical nature of real and financial assets. In the '80s, the equity markets were stagnant so people deemphasized financial assets in favour of real assets. When real assets let them down at the end of the '80s they deemphasized real assets and started loading up on financial assets. When financial assets let them down at the end of the '90s—their behaviour was entirely predictable. They started buying real assets again.

A typical Canadian retiring now will need approximately $500,000 in assets to enjoy a reasonably comfortable retirement and somewhere around double that if they want a prosperous retirement. A house is one of the cornerstones of a sound financial posture. It has obvious benefits with respect to our feelings of security. The issue is not whether real estate is a sound investment but, rather, with the propensity of so many to put so much stock in the house as the sole asset they will rely on for their financial security. It's simply not very prudent to have the full amount of your retirement nest egg in any one asset—especially if it's relatively illiquid and its value is highly cyclical.

Belief No. 3:

The Government Will Look After Me

It has always been a fascination of mine why some people think the government is some autonomous, self-sufficient organization that has an unlimited supply of funds. They seem to think that government exists for the sole purpose of coming to their rescue if something untoward happens—as if it were their own personal safety net. Well, the government IS you. You elect it. You fund it. In this country you own somewhere around a 1/32 millionth share of it. And there are new shareholders being born or immigrating every day. But the government does not really exist to make sure that you enjoy a blissful retirement.

In the '80s and '90s it was pretty common for me to encounter investors who actually believed they were going to exist in retirement on the back of government largess. Thankfully, we don't hear too much about this one any more. There is even a growing proportion of the population who are not even confident the CPP/QPP will still be in existence when they reach retirement. Although I hear a lot less from people who think they will retire solely on government assistance there are still a significant amount of Canadians who believe this to be true.

A FALSE SENSE OF SECURITY

Too many Canadians have an inflated idea of the amount of benefits that CPP provides. A poll by Decima in February 2005 suggested Canadians were pretty much in the dark regarding how much they will get from CPP when they retire. When asked to provide an estimate of how much the CPP paid the average guess was $13,200 compared with the actual amount of $9,945. Interestingly, younger respondents, and those with lower incomes, tended to overestimate the levels of benefits the most.

We live in a prosperous nation and enjoy one of the highest standards of living on the planet. Government schemes alone are largely inadequate to support the average person's lifestyle. These programs were put in place to ensure the elderly did not live in poverty. Their intent was never to provide a comfy retirement—much less a prosperous one. If you are poor the government will continue to take care of you—but don't expect it to be enough to cover your annual golf dues or a significant part of your ambitious travel plans.

Belief No. 4:

I'll Have a Secure Pension

There are approximately 5.5 million Canadians, or 40% of all full-time permanent employees who are part of a company pension plan. Coverage is relatively evenly split between men and women at 41% and 39% respectively.

The three pillars of retirement income for Canadians are personal retirement savings, usually in the form of a personal RRSP, and government transfers such as: CPP, OAS, and GIS and the employer sponsored pension plan.

A GUARANTEED MAYBE

Due to the expense and potential liability of creating and running traditional pension plans small companies typically establish defined contribution pension plans for their employees. These are sometimes referred to as group RRSPs. In these plans only the contributions and not the benefits are guaranteed. This trend is expected to continue as the Canadian economy migrates from a manufacturing base to a service and knowledge based economy. This will place more of an onus on the employees to ensure they become knowledgeable about their plans and make the correct investment choices. This could be as simple as learning about the importance of asset allocation to long-term viability of their retirement plan.

Those who are covered by traditional defined benefit pension plans and think they have nothing to worry about may be in for a rude awakening in the future. In a 2005 report by the Certified General Accountants they estimate the additional funding required to fully fund defined benefit plans has grown from $160 billion in 2003 to $190 billion at the end of 2004. The reason for the under funding has

largely to do with lower rates of return on plan assets mainly attributable to the lower yields on long bonds and the equity markets at the early part of the decade. Currently, companies have a five year period in which to make good on their obligations but would like that extended to ten.

As boomers approach retirement age there will be fewer workers to support them in retirement, which may make the situation even graver. Many of the beneficiaries of these plans; the employees who work in the plants and offices across Canada are largely complacent or ignorant of the situation. They don't understand the threat this situation poses to their retirement security, nor do they have the wherewithal to even know what questions to ask. They simply believe the funds will be there when they retire. And we have all heard or told a story with the words, "Once upon..."

According to the Workplace and Employee Survey, a report by Statistics Canada in 2001, not only can't many employees distinguish between the types of plans, there are also a significant number of employees who think they are covered by a plan when they are not. About half of the full-time permanent private sector employees reported having an RPP or group RRSP; however, 8% were working for firms that had neither type of plan. Of the 2.1 million private sector employees who reported having a group RRSP at work—half a million or roughly a quarter were employed by firms which had no such plan.

Most employees outside of professionals and the senior executives have no idea about their pension plans. Many have access to a group plan but do not know that they have to initiate participation. Perhaps, much of the confusion is attributable to the fact that employees notice the CPP deductions coming off each paycheque and assume they are contributing to the company plan. Believe it or not there are people who think that CPP stands for Company Pension Plan.

There is a crucial need to educate Canadians about the public and private retirement planning systems. This education should include providing simple and accurate information about the characteristics of the plans and realistic projections of the proportion of retirement income they could replace in retirement.

As far as pension plans go there are no guarantees anymore unless you work for the government. They vote themselves the benefits and they have unlimited ability to tax the public. Everyone else has some degree of uncertainty.

Belief No. 5:

My Kids Will Look after Me

A few years ago, on a typical Saturday night my kids were sitting in the family room playing a game while my wife and I were reading. I was looking at my kids and it occurred to me that I had reached middle age and was speeding toward my second childhood. The slippery slope would eventually deliver me to a time where I'd be in diapers again. I didn't mention this vision to my wife. It would have put a damper on the whole virile thing. But the kids were fair game. Someone would have to nurture me. Perhaps, even spoon-feed me. I was thinking, who better to perform those tasks than my own children?

So I asked them, "Are you going to change daddy's diapers when he gets old?" Being somewhat accustomed to my strange sense of humor they just looked at me and calmly replied, "Dad, you're on your own". My wife overheard our conversation. She casually offered to visit me on bingo nights at the institution of her choice. The kids even offered to help her if rotating roles were put in place. So, after further negotiation it was declared that while number dabbing was in—diaper duty was out.

ARRESTED DEVELOPMENT

I often look at my kids and wonder how they will make out in the world as adults. We are having fewer children than in the past but we now indulge them to an extent our parents could not manage or afford. They wear stylish clothing; have the latest, greatest toys and gadgets. Their evenings and weekends are filled with an array of activities we could only dream about when we were their age. We spoil them and protect them to an extent that they scarcely experience criticism or adversity at all. If anything bad should happen to them while they play their computer games they simply hit the "reset" button and they're good to go again. I wonder if this is the reason why the youth of today seem to be delaying their entry into the adult world with all of its related challenges and hazards.

As kids enter adulthood they are increasingly choosing to stay home longer because of the financial benefits. It's a lot cheaper living with mom and dad when they pay for the major expenses like food and shelter. Those tedious tasks like laundry and cleaning are also thrown in for free. According to the 2001 census 41% of the 3.8 million Canadians between the ages of 20 and 29 now live with their parents. This is up from the 27% who lived with mom and dad in 1981.

Many kids are becoming complacent and not using the opportunity to build their financial independence. Rather than practice fiscal responsibility they're opting toward spending their income on luxury goods and exotic vacations. The stigma of living with your parents well into adulthood starts to fade when you're driving around in a great set of wheels. And the free ride really rolls when all your friends are doing it, too.

Part of the reason young people are staying at home longer is they are marrying and starting families of their own much later in life. The median age of first marriage in the early '70s, was 21 for females and 23 for males. By 2001, this had increased dramatically to age 28 and 30 respectively. In 1981, 64% of men and 73% of women between the ages of 25 and 29 were married, but this had declined to 45% of men and 57% of women by 2001. This trend also carried through to parenthood where the median age of a woman having her first baby increased from age 23 to age 28 between 1981 and 2001. When you reach a ripe old age your children may still be having children rather than caring for you.

There has also been an increasing trend toward adults moving back home. According to the 2001 census 33% of men and 28% of women returned to their parent's home at some point after heading out on their own. Like any cultural development it has to be legitimized by a name—so we refer to these people as the 'boomerang generation'. The primary reason for their return is the very reason they were reluctant to leave in the first place—economics. With the divorce rate heading higher, and job tenure heading lower, there is a much greater chance you might be spending a lot more time with Junior in future. Not only might your kids not be in a position to look after you in your old age, they may well be coming to a basement near you.

Belief No. 6:

My Kids Will Get a Scholarship

There are a lot of parents in Canada who have not done enough to save for their children's education. According to Statistics Canada, in 2002 only half of those under the age of 19 had an average of $8600 saved for post secondary education. Factors positively affecting education savings are: higher education and income of parents, home ownership, and high aspirations for children among parents and children who performed well in school. A lack of savings means students will have to assume debt to continue their studies after high school.

Half of all college and bachelor graduates left school owing money, largely in the form of government student loans. In 2000, the average debt of those graduating with a college diploma was $13,000 and for those with bachelor degrees $20,000. Two years after graduation only one in five had paid off their student loans. Those most likely to pay had lower loan amounts and higher post graduate employment income. Far too many of Canada's students are starting their working lives with debt.

MONEY FROM HEAVEN

Scholarships, bursaries, and awards are available to help students deal with the escalating cost of tuition. There are many criteria that may qualify students for upwards of 60,000 annual awards, which range from a couple hundred dollars to several thousand a year. Most are based on academic accomplishments, but there are others that recognize community involvement and the arts. Many students and parents are not even aware of these programs or how to apply for them. Even if you were to qualify for these awards they cannot be relied upon as a source of education funding because there are no guarantees your child will be selected.

The government thinks you should put money away for your children's higher education. To that end, they created the Registered Education Savings Plan (RESP) to facilitate tax-deferred savings. In order to ensure you contribute regularly they also created the Canada Education Savings Grant (CESG) that matches 20% of your contributions up to $400 per year. The grant is even more generous for low income families. According to Statistics Canada families who are aware of the grant program have saved significantly more; it helps when the Feds throw in an extra 20% on every dollar you contribute.

Even if you're not sure your kids will attend a college or university just assume they will because you will be eligible for the CESG and the contributions can be withdrawn or rolled over to an RRSP if they don't go to school.

If saving for your children's education is truly a familial financial stretch; grandparents can be a great help. Many do not have a problem spending money on the grandchildren while their parents wrestle with their careers and a mortgage. A parent can set-up an RESP account for the children, wherein, the grandparents can make the annual contributions on behalf of the parent so none of the grant is lost. If grandparents experience financial hardship they can withdraw their contributions at any time without penalty because they were made with after-tax dollars. The income it generated remains in the plan to the benefit of the children.

The succinct point is: you have to do what is necessary to ensure your children have every opportunity open to them. If your child is bright enough or talented enough to pursue post-secondary education, but has to solely rely on scholarships or a student loan—then it will be harder. Leaving post-secondary education funding to fate could be a fatal financial mistake. It's really not worth the gamble.

Belief No. 7:

I'm Going to Hit the Jackpot

Buying lottery tickets has become a national pastime. In 2002, just over 16 million Canadians or about 65% of the population over the age of 15 reportedly played some form of lottery according to Statscan. Players were pretty evenly split between men and women and geographically representative. Instant win tickets were also played by 9 million Canadians or slightly more than a third of the population over the age of 15. And forty percent of them played one to eleven times per year. For many of them playing the lottery was a harmless exercise where they did not place too much stock in their chances of winning. For others it was a deliberate attempt to pad their retirement nest egg.

DUMB LUCK

I once had the unusual pleasure of meeting a man who was convinced the lottery was going to be the key to his secure retirement. We were having a charming conversation when he dropped his little strategy on me. Of course, I told him that everyone thinks they will win the jackpot but only a very few actually take home the big prize and, perhaps, we should discuss a serious strategy for funding his retirement. He assured me he was different from the rest. When I asked him why he was so sure he would win, he looked at me, and said, "I have a system."

I looked at him and replied, "It's bingo balls coming out of a bingo machine". He assured me that his system would eventually deliver its intended result.

Unbeknownst to me, in his kitchen he had set up a bunch of chalk boards which had numbers all over them. As hard as it was for me to believe, he was very serious about winning the jackpot. I asked him if he would play the combination 1, 2, 3, 4, 5, 6 but, of course, nobody would be so foolish as to play such an obvious loser. I told him that mathematically it had the same chance of winning as any other combination, slim and none. He was not moved. My final attempt to convince him there is no system for winning the lottery was to tell him that the number six does not know that it is his daughter's birthday, and the number 21 does not know that it is his anniversary and the number 42 does not know that it is his street address. If you ask a mathematician they will tell you that numbers have no special meaning or significance—and we cannot impose any on them.

No matter what I said it was not going to spoil his parade. He was going to win even at one in 14 million odds. I often meet people who tell me they have increased their odds by always buying 10 tickets each draw. So you now have a ten in 14 million chance of winning the jackpot. The real problem is the fact that they always hand the jackpot to somebody. The lottery organizers are really good at putting their faces in the press when they come in to pick up their 'freedom' prize. This fuels the dream.

If you think that this scenario is far fetched you would be sadly mistaken. A survey done in 1999 by the Consumer Federation of America and Primerica revealed that approximately 40% of Americans and about half of those in a lower income bracket of $15-$25k a year "thought that winning the lottery would give them their retirement nest egg." Unfortunately, this is a dream held not just by the economically disadvantaged, but also increasingly by those in the middle class. In Canada, almost twice as many who earn more than $20,000 play the lottery than those who earn less than that amount—so it's not just a tax on the poor. It's an equal opportunity social extravaganza—with hopes and an outlay that continually grows more extravagant.

DON'T LET THE JACKPOT HIJACK YOUR DREAM

What's the big deal if someone blows a few dollars on tonight's draw anyway? Well, they don't just play occasionally. Thirty-seven percent of Canadians over the age of 15 played 1 to 7 times a week, twenty-three percent played 1 to 3 times a month and forty percent played 1–11 times a year.

And many of them buy more than one ticket and play more than one draw when the do play. A few dollars here and a few dollars there and, pretty soon, you're talking real money.

The lottery company would not like you to think about this: but if you stopped playing the lottery and saved say $10 a week you would be a lot further ahead. For example, if instead of putting $10 a week into the draw you put that money in a tax-sheltered retirement account earning a modest long term rate of return of 7% it would amount to... $35,000 over twenty five years. If you take the time to figure out how much you've actually personally spent on lotteries over the years and work out an average per month and year, and then calculate how much you would have earned at just a modest rate of return—it's a tidy little jackpot in its own right. I'm not advocating people stop playing the lottery, only that they treat it as the harmless little pastime it was intended to be.

Belief No. 8:

I'll Make It up Later

When you don't have much saved then it seems like you have nothing to lose. But as your savings grow and become more significant you will find that you place a higher premium on protecting your savings. Compounding is like a train that builds momentum. It starts slowly but then it feels like it builds exponentially and before you realize it you have a significant nest egg saved. It's kind of like watching children grow; they seem so young, and then you turn around and they're grown and you're thinking "how did that happen". The secret to savings is time, so the best time to start is now.

Everyone who isn't saving enough or, anything at all, for their future has the same excuse; there isn't enough left at the end of the day. Those of us who were not raised by depression era parents tend to spend what we have and likely a little bit more. Most have never known true hardship and, therefore, have no reason at all to believe they could ever experience any severe economic adversity. The recessions they have experienced have been relatively predictable and largely manageable. If there was any effect on spending it was really nothing more than a little belt-tightening. This makes it easier to think that we will be able to make up for our lack of savings later.

DON'T COMPOUND YOUR PROBLEMS

It has been said that compounding is the 8th wonder of the world.

Those who reach middle age and have not saved very much have the same alibi; I'll power save later when my financial obligations are less onerous and I'm making more money. This is the psychological free pass they keep in their hip pocket. It allows them to go on spending without the guilt. They might actually even do this, but the point is: they will have wasted an incredible opportunity to have their savings compound over time. The easiest way I can explain this is to tell people the strategy of starting late is like simple addition where you are adding sums of money. On the other hand saving and investing early is like multiplication where each sum grows exponentially.

Many advisors will tell their clients to first pay off debt before saving. I don't generally tell people to do this. The reason is because many of the people I've met have been incredibly accomplished spenders. They never seem to get out of debt, certainly not in a very efficient way. Telling them to stop spending is like fighting a very strong current. The best way to save is to put aside some of every paycheque automatically. It may not be much in the early years when you are establishing yourself and expenses are larger, but make sure it is something. There is no right age. Start as soon as you have some income.

Belief No. 9:

I'm Healthy So I Don't Need Insurance

Everywhere around us there are possibilities and probabilities. The possibilities, positive and negative, are infinite, but it is the probabilities that will largely determine how real the possibilities are. If things are going good now we tend to believe they will be good forever. After all, bad things don't happen to us. They happen to other people we read or hear about in the news. The reason we don't naturally think anything bad will happen to us is because the odds are they won't. So, we go on thinking all is well without the need to take precautions. But what if we're wrong? How bad could it be and what are the chances?

According to the National Safety Council, every year 1 out of every 88 homes will catch fire, while 1 in 70 motor vehicles are involved in an accident causing disability, injury or death. Everyone has car insurance because it is legally mandated and no lender will give you a mortgage without house insurance. But we don't typically purchase critical illness or disability insurance even thought the odds are great that we may suffer a setback. The probabilities are that 3 in 10 healthy male adults and 2.7 in 10 healthy female adults will have a critical illness before age 65. When the decision of whether or not to insure is left up to us—we often don't do what the probabilities state we should.

SAY HELLO TO MURPHY

Murphy's Law: "if anything can go wrong, it will" was not meant as a nihilist rallying cry invented by some morose character. Capt. Edward A. Murphy was an engineer in the US Air Force working on dangerous projects. Because of the nature of his work the phrase came to be accepted by he and his colleagues as a way to ensure they had taken every precaution to ensure the safety of all those involved. This means doing the things that are most likely to produce the desired effect, while avoiding the activities which are likely to lead to disaster. Today the phrase is often used in a fatalistic sense, but Capt. Murphy would never have left things to chance, he would have been prepared for every outcome.

Some of the excuses we use not to buy insurance include, "My wife will remarry", "God won't let anything bad happen to me", "I have insurance at work", and "I'm healthy so I don't need it". Add the fact most people don't enjoy thinking about their mortality or bodily harm, or dealing with insurance agents, and you can see why we make excuses or procrastinate, that is, until the unthinkable happens. The problem with insurance is you cannot retroactively purchase it. You need to purchase it while things are going great. It is, essentially, a bet against our well being that is really worth taking.

Sorrow and anxiety are the emotional byproducts of adversity, and loss of income is the economic price. You may not have complete control of the first but you can manage the second. It strikes me as odd that many of us won't buy insurance to mitigate the financial effects of unfortunate illness or death but we have no problem buying lottery tickets with astronomical odds against winning. The first line of defense in risk management is to simply be aware of what could go wrong and what effect it could have on you and your family. Once you have done this; you can make intelligent decisions on how best to protect your possessions and yourselves.

Belief No. 10:

I Can't Wait Till I Retire—Then I'll Be Happy

It's not surprising that many of us hold this belief. Work can often seem like a grind and there may be family responsibilities that prevent us from doing the things we would like to do. Advertising seems to be the driver of much of our current dissatisfaction. Financial Services companies are always running those ads which show people who are supposed to be like us doing all kinds of exciting activities. In the ads we're always smiling and laughing as we tighten the sail or hit that perfect golf shot. I never knew I loved yachting so much! And right now I only smile after one in ten golf shots. So, personally, I'm really looking forward to retirement.

MAKE SURE YOUR FAREWELL PARTY IS NOT THE HILIGHT OF YOUR RETIREMENT

At the point of retirement you will be entering a period of dramatic change. By the time retirement rolls around we've been in the working world for the majority of our lives. Work has been a big part of our routine and has largely defined who we are. One of the first questions we are asked when we meet a new acquaintance is, "What do you do?" We don't ask what they mean by that, we simply tell them what our occupation is.

Psychologically, leaving work may not be as easy as we presume. Many take their sense of identity from their work. A great deal of our social interaction including many of our friends and even some of our spouses were derived from work. Once we retire many things change and for some it may be a difficult adjustment. Loss of identity, boredom, and loneliness are some of the common problems that face retirees.

PLAN NOTHING AND YOU'LL DO NOTHING

Some people have told me they're going to do absolutely nothing when they retire—just because they can. Therefore, they don't need to plan what they're going to do in their retirement. I've met a lot of retirees who've scheduled their lives around various doctors' appointments. Sometimes it's nice to have to be somewhere when you don't have to be somewhere. Planning what you're going to do in retirement is kind of like going on a vacation. If you don't plan to do anything then you end up doing nothing. If that's cool with you then OK. But many of you will find that awfully boring and very unsatisfying.

NO ONE HAS EVER ESCAPED DEATH

With the possible exception of Elvis, no one has ever managed to avoid dying. Some people have had their crucial bits frozen and expect to come back to life some day but no matter who we are we all know how the story ends. We can die suddenly but most of us will gradually deteriorate until our ticket finally gets punched and we get on the Netherworld Express. However, due to modern science the flight keeps getting delayed. But will we really want to hang around the departure lounge that long? At least Elvis got to leave the building.

In those retirement ads we're never in a wheelchair with tubes coming out of our nose. They always show us on the first day of retirement when we're still fit and foolish. But there is another side to retirement that you don't see in those ads, the part where you are frail and need extensive care; where your grandchildren don't seem to be around as much because they have full lives of their own, and you're just not as much fun as you used to be before you had to be helped out of a car, or to be fed. You need to be aware that there will likely be a period of your life where you may not be active at all.

Irrespective of how satisfied with our lives we are now, I think much of the reason we believe that retirement will be a better life has to do with the way in which we look at the adult life stages. Each period; education, work and retirement are psychologically viewed by many of us as periods where we first do what we have to do, followed by doing what we need to do, and finally doing what we want to do. But life is seldom that clear cut and we don't always get to do what we want to do because of physical, emotional or economic constraints. Even if all the stars align and we get to do what we want to do it may not bring us the contentment we had hoped for.

Make sure your longing for retirement isn't a reflection of something that is terribly lacking in your life right now. You cannot live in the future just hoping it will be a better life. It's as futile as living in the past. We think that "all's well that ends well" will be our salvation, but you shouldn't wait to be happy. For all the people who told me they were waiting for retirement to bring happiness it always occurred to me that it might make more sense to work on their current level of happiness and shoot for comfort now.

I have only examined a few of the more common money myths or beliefs that I have observed over the years. There must be dozens, or even hundreds of money beliefs out there that drive our motivations and behavior. It is not important whether or not you recognize one of these as applying to you, only that you realize that you are likely guided by some money precept, which may or may not be truly personal to you. If you think they have compromised your sense of financial security resolve to do something. If nothing else, get help. It's never too late.

Too many people regard their financial future as a threat. But the future is much less of a threat if you prepare for it. Securing your income, saving a portion of it, owning your home and planning early for retirement are the keys to achieving financial security for most Canadians. If you do all of these things there is a virtual certainty that you will be OK.

OK Home*Work*Book

WHAT IS YOUR BIGGEST FINANCIAL FEAR?

WHAT ARE YOUR BIGGEST FINANCIAL REGRETS?

WHO TAUGHT YOU ABOUT MONEY?

DO YOU CONSIDER YOURSELF CAUTIOUS OR CARELESS WITH YOUR FINANCES?

___

___

___

WHAT IS YOUR DEFINITION OF FINANCIAL SECURITY (ECONOMIC AND EMOTIONAL)?

___

___

___

___

WHAT IS THE PRIMARY OBJECTIVE OF YOUR FINANCIAL PLAN?

___

___

___

___

DO YOU FEEL THAT YOU HAVE CHOSEN THE RIGHT CAREER?

WHAT HAVE YOU DONE TO SECURE YOUR INCOME?

HOW DO YOU PLAN TO CONTROL DEBT?

WHAT IS YOUR FINANCIAL DROP DEAD DATE?

WHAT WOULD YOU CONSIDER AN ADEQUATE EMERGENCY FUND?

DO YOU OWN A HOUSE OR DO YOU OWN A MORTGAGE?

WHEN WILL YOUR MORTGAGE BE PAID?

WHAT IS THE CURRENT EQUITY IN YOUR HOME?

WHAT IS YOUR CURRENT LEVEL OF FINANCIAL ASSETS?

HOW BALANCED ARE YOUR FINANCIAL ASSETS AND REAL ASSETS?

WHAT DOES YOUR IDEAL RETIREMENT LOOK LIKE?

WHAT HAVE YOU DONE TO REALIZE YOUR RETIREMENT DREAM?